PRAISE FOR CLIMBING FASTER, STRONGER, HEALTHIER

"Vital information! I wish I had this information when I began climbing. There is such a gold mine of information here that it almost feels like cheating."
–Fred Beckey: Author of The Cascade Alpine Guide series, Range of Glaciers, Challenge of the North Cascades, Mount McKinley: Icy Crown of North America, The Bugaboos: An Alpine History, and one of the most accomplished climbers to ever have lived.

"Climbers of all disciplines will find this a valuable resource for improving their fitness, skill and performance. It is packed with useful information that is a reflection of Mike's broad experiences as both an alpinist and a health care professional."
-Mark Westman: Accomplished Alaskan extreme alpinist

"I like what I see…spoken in a voice of someone both determined to help others learn and someone with insight. The ground cover[ed] is enormous. This is not a chest thumping attempt to show off what you know. It is an honest, provocative analysis of what a serious climber should be thinking about 365 days a year. Seasoned climbers may or may not agree with every sentence in this expansive coverage. But no one can argue that you have offered a series of topics that every climber should eventually delve into if they wish to reach the highest levels of the discipline." *–Carlos Buhler: Author for National Geographic, motivational speaker, extreme high-altitude alpinist, recipient of the Underhill Award, Mugs Stump Award, and the Spitzer Award.*

"Layton nailed it! This book is destined to become the bible on climbing stronger, faster, and healthier. No other book on these subjects offers such thorough and up to date information. Dr. Layton has written the 'New Testament' for climbers."
-Jim Nelson: Author of "Selected Climbs in the North Cascades" Volumes I & II, owner of Pro Mountain Sports, and accomplished first ascensionist.

"An incredible resource for every climber's library. Dr. Layton's expertise as an accomplished climber and as an excellent doctor really shows."
–Cameron Burns: Author of "Selected Climbs of the Desert Southwest", "Climbing Colorado's Fourteeners", "Kilimanjaro& East Africa: Climbing and Trekking Guide", "Colorado Ice Climber's Guide", and pioneer of hundreds of desert climbs.

"Layton's years of mountain experience and passion absolutely shine through. It's a boiled down encyclopedia of absolute best-climbing-practices that can only have been gleaned from years on the sharp-end of all varieties of mountain environment. Layton has landed on a winning recipe of delivering the full package to the modern climber. This book is all about providing climbers of all types with the most efficient, logical and thoughtful methods of improving your vertical game, and the trick is to read these sections as you need to build that strength. There's an endless flow of nuggets that just can't be gained from any other way (up until now!) than by suffering through the trials and tribulations of the sharp end. Even the most experienced ropeguns and hardened mountaineers will be able to glean some gems from this collection of wisdom."
–Lyle Knight: Author of "Central BC Rock: The Rockclimbers Guide to Central British Columbia", and accomplished climber.

"I recently had the privilege to review "Climbing Stronger Faster, Healthier" The content is incredibly valuable. As an outdoor adventure writer and climbing guide, I believe that Mike's book will fill a niche that is not currently receiving a lot of attention. Mike is an incredibly accomplished alpinist and those who have suffered through any type of alpine climb – be it an ascent on Mount Rainier or an extreme route in Alaska – are always looking to people like him for more ways to train and more tips for "high-end" ascents…I can assure you that it will be added to the reading list for American Alpine Institute clients. I imagine that other guide services will do the same throughout the United States in Canada."
-Jason Martin: Author of "Washington Ice: A Climber's Guide", professional playwright, accomplished mountain guide, and Director of the American Alpine Institute.

"Dr. Mike Layton has been a friend and colleague for several years now and to this day it still amazes me the amount of knowledge and passion for climbing that this man has! Not only does his passion for climbing fuel his own athletic aspirations but also, it fuels his desire to help others achieve what he has through proper planning and preparation for an ascent. On the pages of this book you will find invaluable information on how to be more prepared for the task at hand and you will find that even though climbing, while seemingly rudimentary, can be as involved as you wish it to be!"
-Erik DeRoche MS, DC, CSCS: Chiropractic sports physician, professional triathlete, co-owner of Run Without Limits.

"Concise, comprehensive, and informative. Everything a modern, do-it-yourself alpine athlete needs to succeed. I wish all of my patients would use this book and wouldn't end up in the ER in the first place."
-Erik Denninghoff, M.D.: Emergency Room Physician and Climber.

Cascade Pass, Washington

Climbing Stronger, Faster, Healthier: *Beyond the Basics*

First Edition: Second Printing: November, 2009

Cover and Book Design by: Michael Layton
Illustrations (pages 161, 172, 173, 174) by Zac Reisner - Copyright 2009 by the Illustrator.
All Photos by: Michael Layton unless otherwise noted.
Cover Photo by John Scurlock: *The Haunted Wall on Spectre Peak. Southern Picket Range, North Cascades Washington.*
Back Cover: *Ice Climbing on Stairway to Heaven, UT. Michael Layton Photo. Rock Climbing at Smith Rock State Park, OR. Photo courtesy of Ian Roth.*

ISBN: 1-4392-3198-2

<u>For additional copies and updated information</u>
Homepage: http://sites.google.com/site/climbingstronger
Email: climbingstronger@hotmail.com

Southern Pickets, WA

CLIMBING STRONGER, FASTER, HEALTHIER: *BEYOND THE BASICS*

Michael A. Layton, D.C.

Bells Canyon, Utah
Brian Waters Photo

Lone Peak Cirque, Utah

CONTENTS

ACKNOWLEDGEMENTS

I want to sincerely thank the following people who helped this book become a reality: Adam Riser, Alan Kearney, The Guides at the American Alpine Institute, Angela Hawse, Anne Arnoldy, ARUP Laboratories, Ashley George, Bill Mullee, Blake Herrington, Brian Eckerling, Brian Thomas, D.C., Brian Waters, Britne Gose, Cameron Burns, Carlos Buhler, www.cascadeclimbers.com., Chris Chlebowski, D.C., N.D., Cory Bennett, Darin Berdinka, Eric Denninghoff, M.D., Eric Linthewaite, Eric Wehrly, Eric Wolfe, Erik DeRoche, D.C., Feathered Friends, Fred Beckey, The Front Climbing Club, Garth Sundem, Gavin Ferguson, Graham Williams and Cilogear, Graston Technique®, Heart Rate Incorporated, Ian Roth, I.M.E. in Salt Lake City, James Arnold. James Claxton, James Garrett, R.N., Jason Martin, Jay Hack, Jim Nelson and Pro Mountain Sports, Joe Josephson, John Frieh, John Scurlock, Josh Kaplan, Justin Thibault, Kathleen Cartmell, Lane Brown, La Sportiva, Lyle Knight, Mark Allen, Mark Westman, Marcus Donaldson, Marmot, Meditech International, Melissa McClone, Metolius, Mike Powers, My Family, Nick Doleck, Peter Hirst, Petzl, Radek Chalupa, Rolf Larson, Salt Lake Running Company, Tyler Adams, The Teachers at Western States Chiropractic College and Western Washington University, Wayne Wallace, Wild Country, Zac Reisner (whose illustrations are works of art) and all my climbing partners past, future, and present for teaching me all I wrote in this book that wasn't pure trial and error on my part.

Enchantments, WA
Mark Allen Photo

FOREWORD
BY WAYNE WALLACE

Few authors are capable of capturing in words that passion that can come from the experience of climbing. Writing is one of the last things that I think of when I am exposed to this truly amazing game. For me, writing is much more difficult than climbing. Yet it was reading the great books on climbing that shaped my early interest, and in what would soon become a big part of my life-long story. Learning from books as an elementary student taught me vital techniques, and sparked further interest in what seemed like an unreachable subject. Later, when I began viewing myself as an athlete, books helped target and refine my efforts. I learned that if you are smart, you don't have to be as tough. Unreachable goals could be reached if you had the knowledge. The more knowledge you have as a climber, the harder you can climb. The more you can break down unimaginable tasks into pieces, the simpler they appear. To most, this was learned the hard way – through trial and error.

As the Northwest climbing scene ramped up in the new century after a decade of stagnation, it became apparent with each new climb, that Mike Layton was not just a lucky climber. In fact, after a huge amount of failures (he once approached a climb with a two day approach SIX TIMES!), his abilities, knowledge and passion have carried him and anyone associated with him to the top of what the climbing life can offer. His relentless success on big, new routes has hit legendary status. It is not easy to find a partner with as much hunger for such tough, wild climbs. It is also almost impossible to find someone who can endure such willingness to admit defeat, suffer endlessly, carry more than his weight, push himself further than his body should allow, and yet care more about the friendships that are created.

I remember once when we were fully beaten – I mean whipped – and he cracked a smile and made a joke so stupid that we both forgot what horrible mess we were in. Instead of giving up, he suggested we start again....after eight hours of bushwacking through thorn bushes in the rain, and wading in and out of a freezing river. Together, we made an impossible situation possible. And together, we free-climbed a big wall on the most remote peak in the lower 48 after a full day horrific false start. This is someone you ought to at least take a few notes from....

The alter ego of Mike's personality is his profession in the field of medicine. As a patient of his, I have seen his depth of care he has for all people truly interested in helping and improving their bodies. I can't think of anyone more suited to the task than a person as devoted as Mike (although if you met him in the mountains you would never guess to call him "Doctor Layton").

You are about to read a thesis that will condense decades of climbing experience soaked in by one of the great teachers of climbing. Each chapter is really its own book. My favorite aspect of this book is the "geekery" of climbing tips and tricks that have never been in a climbing book (until now!).

Climbing is the best opportunity to do the truly amazing for the average person. It is a diverse sport that openly accepts all genders, ambitions, and backgrounds. It offers exotic travel, adventure, fitness, and a vast social network. A primitive void is satisfied in this modern and convenience oriented society.

This sport may or may not hold as much of your attention as it has mine, but either way, it is in your best interest to learn as much as possible about it if you are going to play this somewhat dangerous and eclectic pursuit. Being a more savvy and fit climber is not only safer, but success is greatly increased without the added struggle of being out-of-shape.

It is not easy to recognize opportunities at the time they are granted. They are usually clouded by the emotions that come from looming change. Careful thought is required. Haunting questions must be answered. Do you really want to do the upper echelon climbs? Are you up for the drudgery of a fitness routine? I hope you make a few positive choices while reading ahead. I hope you choose to make the highest commitment to the safety and well being to yourself and the people that make your life possible. I hope you make the personal commitment to reach out and grab the highest and best that is available in this short life.

This book will assume a few things. You have not only answered yes to the questions above you are salivating over every word you are reading! You have already learned the basics. You intend to honor your time invested here and be accountable for it. You are ready to do the climbs that most can only dream about.

You are about to equip yourself with the final tools that can make these dreams come true. I enthusiastically support sharing your stories with us along the way!

Wayne Wallace.
Seattle, Washington. June 9, 2009

Icefields Parkway, Canada

Enchantments, Washington

INTRODUCTION

This began as a "no-fluff" outline of a climber's training regimen, but it evolved into a whole lot more. Unless you have access to excellent local climbing and countless partners, a lot of the skill and muscle you develop will be lost between periods of climbing. This is why training is necessary to not only get better at climbing, but to maintain the level you are currently climbing at. Otherwise, your climbing skill level will either look like a roller coaster of ups and downs, or just a plateau at your current level. Training doesn't just mean lifting weights or bouldering in the gym. It also means disciplining yourself by learning new skills, practicing old ones, and taking care of your body. Climbing places stress on your body in repetitive ways it may not be used to. Training helps to get your body used to all the weird positions and stress involved, but sometimes the inevitable occurs: you get an injury. These injuries are more commonly repetitive overuse injuries than the emergency room type.

Beginning climbers will benefit from almost all of these exercises and tips. However, technique and mileage are the most crucial elements at this beginner's stage. This manual doesn't come close for substituting technique and skill. I have included a section on injuries and nutrition, drawing on my experience as a chiropractic physician, and a section on climbing equipment, nutrition, and tips gained from lots of climbing partners, epics, and ideas gained from way too many trips into the hills. This book should help you where the standard learning to climb books leave off. I have included a list of other additional helpful texts at the end of the book.

Every piece of equipment in this book has undergone extreme scrutiny and field testing under the harshest conditions by my climbing partners and me. I apologize if any return policies were changed as a result. As new equipment evolves and old attitudes change, I hope to include the future in outdoor gear as it relates to climbing and mountain travel. I did not receive a single dollar or ANY free gear for any ads or product endorsements in this book. If you are a gear manufacturer, I challenge you to create useful products for inclusions in future editions. Many customer service bridges were burned while writing this book in the sole interest of the reader.

Being a doctor of chiropractic has been extremely difficult for me. My goal in treatment has always been to offer the least invasive, most effective, cheapest, and most up to date methods possible because that's what I've always wanted as a patient. It wasn't until I started practicing that I realized the stigma, even bigotry that surrounded my profession. Since I cannot perform surgery or prescribe drugs, but am considered a primary care physician, I am forced by my own practical limitations to help people in the ways I originally intended. However, the good news is that this is what people really want! So, to those who don't "believe" in my profession, please pretend that someone else is giving this advice! Unless you need surgery or meds, the tools to get better from almost all climbing injuries are included within. There is nothing mystical, new age, or unscientific advice included in this book. I think you'll be surprised at what I don't recommend versus what I do. I have always been my biggest skeptic.

Even though this book is relatively short, I think you'll find that there is so much information in here, you will probably need to read it once, go over it again with a highlighter (and maybe Google to look up unfamiliar words – sorry no glossary), practice some of the information, and then read it again. Even though I wrote this, I don't have all the information memorized! I plan on owning a copy myself and using it as a reference.

FEEDBACK

I would greatly appreciate any feedback on the subject matter contained in this book. If there is a topic you would like to see in the next edition, you have a difference of opinion on the subject matter, have new ideas on gear, or have any ideas or comments you would like to share for new editions.

You can also email me if you'd like to be included in an occasional newsletter, or if you will be in Salt Lake City and would like to be evaluated or treated by me. Hopefully you've learned at least one trick or exercise that will improve your climbing from reading this book. The entire book was written, edited, designed, and published by yours truly. Thanks again to all who contributed.

Please send emails to: *climbingstronger@hotmail.com* or visit http://sites.google.com/site/climbingstronger

Sincerely,

Michael A. Layton, D.C.
September 7, 2009. Salt Lake City, Utah.

CHAPTER ONE: TRAINING

Red Rocks, Nevada

HOW TO TRAIN

Let's face it, for most people training is a royal pain in the butt. It cuts into valuable climbing time, creates injuries without actually climbing something, sucks up your time, and sometimes is just incredibly boring. So why train? Some of the world's most genetically gifted climbers don't ever train – they just climb and get better through experience and mileage. But we're not among the world's top climbers…yet. For those of us who aren't genetically or financially pre-disposed to being world class climbers, we need to train to get better, unless you're totally happy with climbing at your current level. But so many great routes require a level of fitness we don't have just yet. Perhaps there's a climb you've always wanted to do, but just aren't ready for yet? Maybe you're sick of starting over at the beginning of every season? Or maybe you just want to get strong, or become a healthier person? If any of these struck a chord with you, read on. It's time to hit the gym!

This is a 22 week (5 month) intensive training routine. There are several great training books on climbing out there, but I wrote this to create an easy to follow routine that any type or level of climber can benefit from. While other books leave what exercises to do and how to do them up to a myriad amount of schedule and periodization graphs, I designed this to follow a specific program. However, it is customizable in that you don't have to do every exercise. I felt there was too much ambiguity in other training books, so hopefully this one will be straightforward and easy to follow.

What won't be easy is actually take the time to do the exercises! The program outlined below is extremely demanding, requiring about 10 hours per week of training at the gym, the wall, crag, or outside. If you can, find a climbing gym that offers at least some basic equipment to train on to make better use of your time. No matter what your discipline of climbing is: bouldering, sport, trad, or ice – the same general rules of training apply. If you are an alpinist, focus on lower body, cardio, and general muscle groups with less emphasis on finger strength. Ice climbers can use ice tools for pull ups, and climb juggier/longer routes for training. Sport climbers may want to skimp on the lower body and cardio exercises.

Never follow an intense workout with one that works the same muscles the next day! In fact, try and schedule at least two days rest after an intense session on a set of major muscle groups. If you do slack off and skip a work-out, do not make it up if it breaks the two to three day rest rule for the more intense exercises. Move on to the next set of exercises. If you have a specific climbing season or big trip planned, start four to five months before you want to be prepared.

> **Begin Training Early February**= Peak date of the beginning of July.
> **Late August start** = Beginning of January peak.

Once you've gone through one cycle of training and taken a good solid rest, training for winter or summer will now only take 10 weeks. If you're climbing at an elite level with an extremely high level of fitness and strength, the training cycle is only 6 weeks. So it makes sense to not slack off, because the work you do now will build a lifelong foundation. Obviously any injury and sickness will delay your schedule. If this happens and you can recover in less than a couple weeks, just add a couple more weeks to your training - don't try and make it up! That is a guaranteed way to make your injury worse. You can't play "catch-up" with training because the change of injury increases drastically. If life happens and something comes up that will physically or emotionally distract you from continuing with your training, all is not lost. Do your best and try to be creative on how to get in your workouts. Do your squats while you brush your teeth if necessary. If you have limited time, work your weaknesses within the weekly progression instead of jumping back and forth between stages.

Be sure to work your non-climbing muscles at least once a week. Keep track of what muscle groups you've been using, and remember to work the others the next time. If you do too much at once, you <u>will</u> get injured. The supporting tissues to your muscles (fascia, ligaments, tendons and cartilage) need time to respond to the new stresses put upon them. It is impossible to do every one of the exercises on a weekly basis without becoming injured or burnt-out. Keep a training journal, even if it's just putting each day's training sheet in a folder with what you did checked off. Write down as much as you can about that day's training: whether it was that you needed to practice footwork, you thought you were getting better, or you needed to do more outdoor climbing. Then look back at what you wrote each week and see if something that needs to be changed for the next week. Injuries and training go hand in hand, even if you aren't over training.

If you develop pain or a problem in any area, STOP, and rethink your plan. You may just need a break, or there may be a biomechanical flaw in your technique. This is why it's a great idea to find a training partner to critique your form, and to motivate and add creativity to your schedule. Try your best and stick to this program.

A few minor modifications are usually all that is necessary. A great way to make sure you do your exercises is at the beginning of each training week, write out every single warm up, cool down, stretch, exercise, run, and climb (including the grade and type of climb), on a piece of paper for every day. Stick with it and don't be afraid to try! Do not rush your work-out. Fuel you body before, during, and after the work out. Warm-up. Cool-down. Finally, do your stretches after instead of rushing home. Have fun, and good luck!

Begin and end every training session with a Warm-Up and a Cool Down

> **Warm-up.** 10-20 minutes light cardio or easy climbing.
> **Cool-down.** 5-10 minutes light cardio after each workout and 20 minutes stretching all involved muscle groups.

Bored? Mix it up
Take occasional forays into the next or previous phase of training to mix it up and overcome training plateaus.

Be Creative
The exercises here are just general guidelines. Train with a partner. Play add-on, down-climb, blindfold, etc...

Breathing
Keeping your shoulders down, breathe in through your nose and expand your belly during the lowering phase. Now breathe out through your mouth slowly while drawing your stomach in by engaging your transverse abdominals while in the lifting, pushing, or pulling phase.

SOME DEFINITIONS

Isometric Contraction
An isometric contraction means to hold a contraction at an isolated, specific angle or position for a length of time. Climbing utilizes isometric muscle contractions quite a bit, so it makes sense to train in a similar fashion. You can fall off a route because you can't pull yourself up it, but it's usually because you can't hold on any longer. Unfortunately, an isometric hold only trains the muscle in a 20 degree range up or down from where you're holding the weight. To make it easier, use the most common positions which are: fully extended (180 degrees), locked off (0 degrees), and 90 degrees. The most difficult position to maintain is just short of fully extended (about 120 degrees) and is mentioned in specific exercises.

Concentric Contraction
This means to lift an object against gravity, like a biceps curl or a pull-up. This type of contraction is usually used to gain upwards progress on the climb.

Eccentric Contraction
This type of muscle contraction is used to lower or decelerate an object against gravity. *For example: lowering from a pull-up, running downhill, or lowering a weight after a biceps curl.* This is the most injury-prone way to use a muscle and it creates soreness. Most muscle damage and micro trauma occurs with this phase of contraction. Training for this type of contraction will help reduce soreness and injury while climbing, but the training itself can burn for days.

Plyometrics
Plyometric contractions are sudden bursts of strength from a resting position. These exercises include such activities as tossing a medicine ball, clean and jerks, dynamic lunges, and muscle-ups (a Cross-Fit exercise). These are extremely functional exercises, and have been applied to the climbing exercises that benefit from this type of muscle contraction. Dynamic climbing movements like dynos and lunges are plyometric type movements. Jumping drills and medicine ball toss exercises are excellent Plyometric exercises, but are not necessarily climbing specific. If you manage to have left over time (good luck!) feel free to do some of these exercises. Exercise books relating to quick burst type sports (like basketball) are good recourses.

Proprioception
Proprioception is you body's awareness of the position your joints are in space. This is an extremely important aspect of training as it builds balance, reduces injury, and streamlines movement saving valuable energy.

Failure
Lifting a weight until failure means that you are unable to lift the weight through the complete range of motion.

Max
This is the most amount of weight you can lift. You should only able to fully complete one repetition before failure. Have a spotter handy and don't attempt to "max out" to find the correct weight for each exercise in a single day!

Reps
Short for repetitions, or how many times you can lift the weight (usually just before failure).

Sets
One cycle of reps, with a rest to follow.

Pit of Despair – Ruth George, Alaska
Cory Bennett Photo

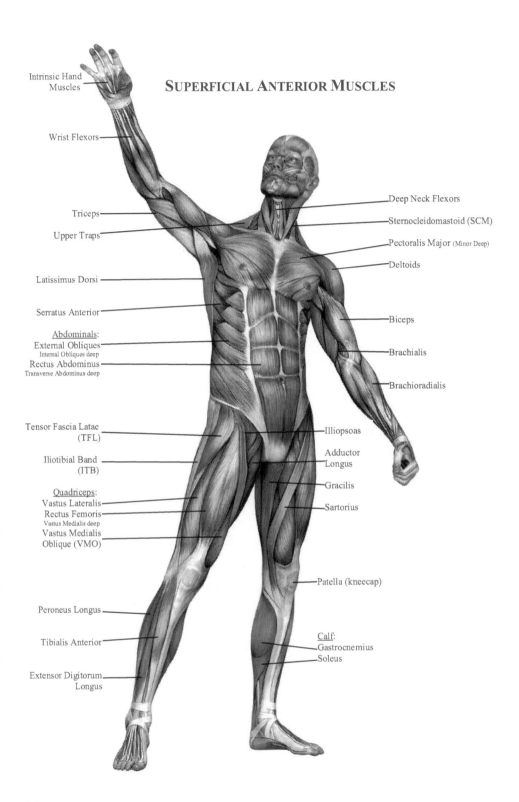

SUPERFICIAL ANTERIOR MUSCLES

Intrinsic Hand Muscles

Wrist Flexors

Triceps

Upper Traps

Latissimus Dorsi

Serratus Anterior

Abdominals:
External Obliques
Internal Obliques deep
Rectus Abdominus
Transverse Abdominus deep

Tensor Fascia Latae (TFL)

Iliotibial Band (ITB)

Quadriceps:
Vastus Lateralis
Rectus Femoris
Vastus Medialis deep
Vastus Medialis Oblique (VMO)

Peroneus Longus

Tibialis Anterior

Extensor Digitorum Longus

Deep Neck Flexors

Sternocleidomastoid (SCM)

Pectoralis Major (Minor Deep)

Deltoids

Biceps

Brachialis

Brachioradialis

Illiopsoas

Adductor Longus

Gracilis

Sartorius

Patella (kneecap)

Calf:
Gastrocnemius
Soleus

SUPERFICIAL POSTERIOR MUSCLES

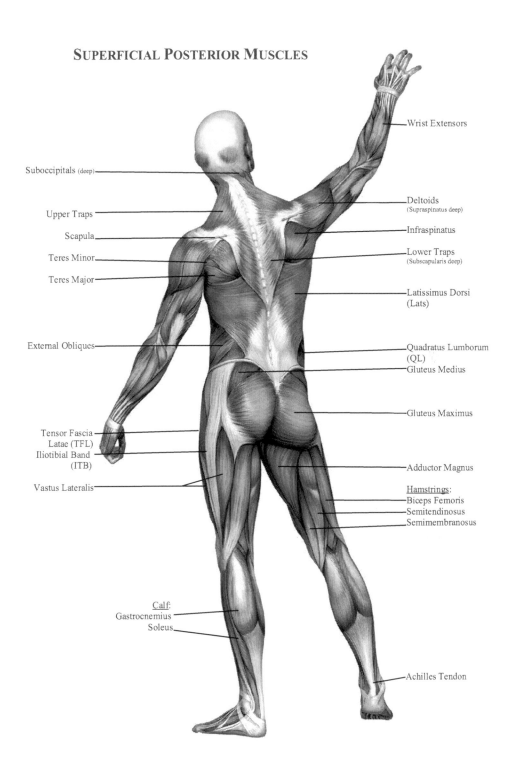

Wrist Extensors

Suboccipitals (deep)

Upper Traps

Scapula

Teres Minor

Teres Major

External Obliques

Tensor Fascia
Latae (TFL)
Iliotibial Band
(ITB)

Vastus Lateralis

Calf:
Gastrocnemius
Soleus

Deltoids
(Supraspinatus deep)

Infraspinatus

Lower Traps
(Subscapularis deep)

Latissimus Dorsi
(Lats)

Quadratus Lumborum
(QL)

Gluteus Medius

Gluteus Maximus

Adductor Magnus

Hamstrings:
Biceps Femoris
Semitendinosus
Semimembranosus

Achilles Tendon

MUSCLES OF THE BACK: SUPERFICIAL AND DEEP

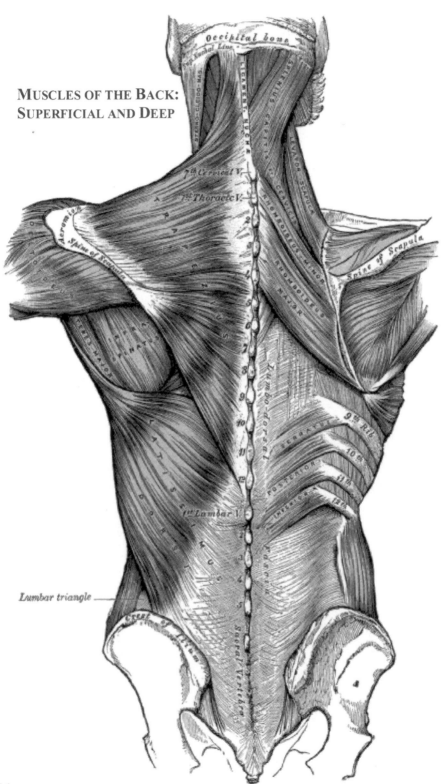

Lumbar triangle

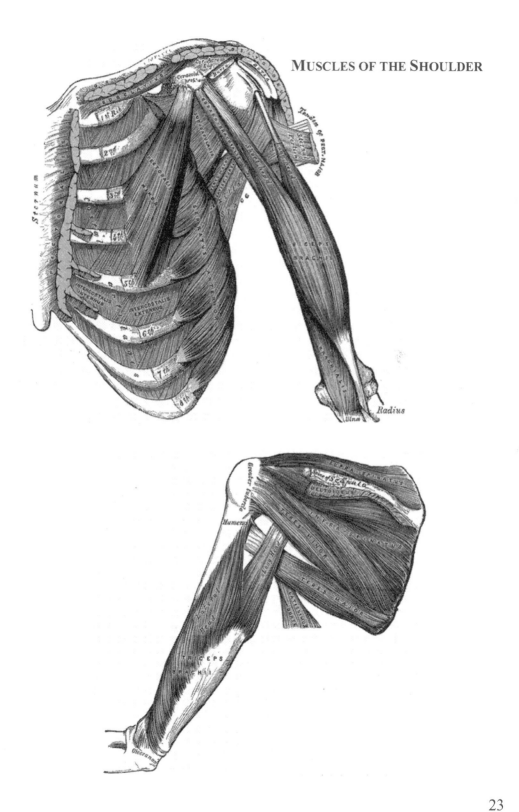

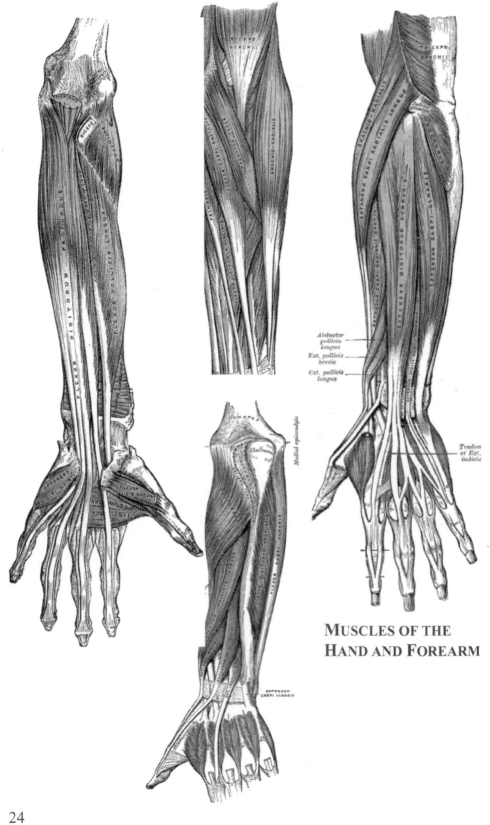

**MUSCLES OF THE
HAND AND FOREARM**

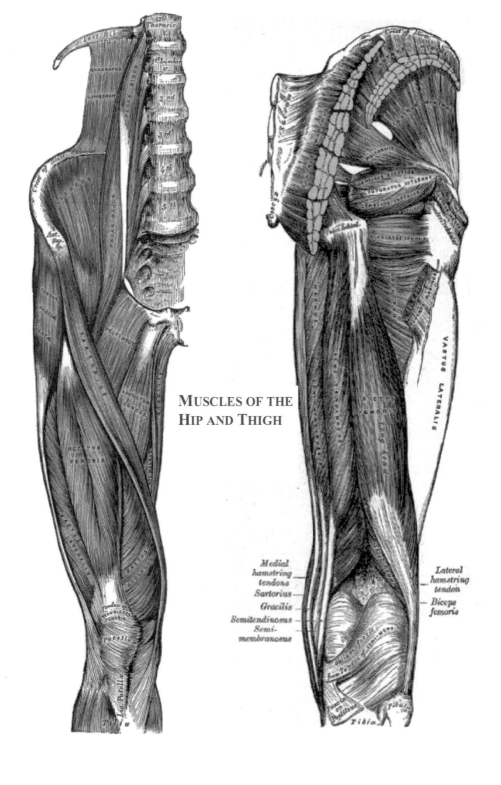

MUSCLES OF THE HIP AND THIGH

Medial
hamstring
tendons
Sartorius
Gracilis
Semitendinosus
Semi-
membranosus

Lateral
hamstring
tendon
Biceps
femoris

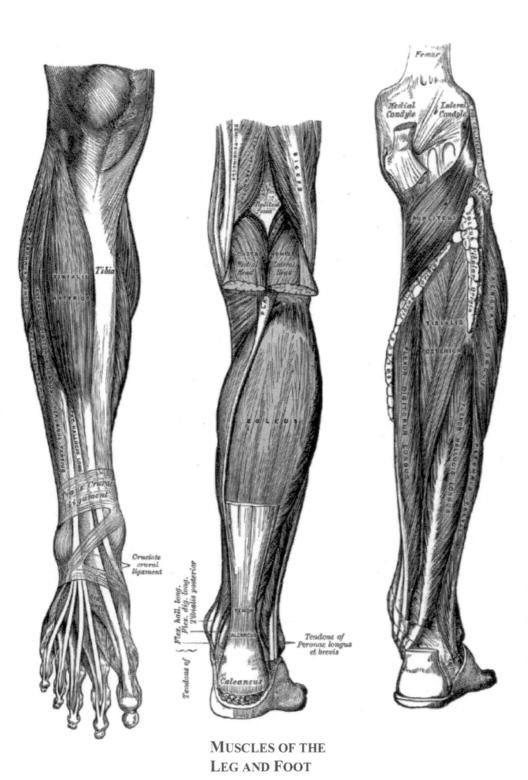

MUSCLES OF THE LEG AND FOOT

CLIMBING SPECIFIC EXERCISES

Training for climbing by actually going climbing is by far the best way to improve. If you have to sacrifice a routine, don't make it climbing! Described below are four different stages of climbing specific training. The **Foundation** climbing exercises are meant to build up a baseline of climbing fitness through mileage, technique, and general strength gains. Once your body has adapted, you're going to plateau or improve very slowly. This is where most weekend warrior climbers remain. Now that the muscles are primed and ready, it's time to build more strength. This is the **Hypertrophy** stage, or muscle growth stage. An untrained muscle will not utilize all of its fibers, no matter how big it is. Once you've built more muscles, you need to use them to their full potential, and that's where the **Maximum Recruitment** phase becomes important. If you're going to have muscles, might as well use as many muscle fibers as you can with each contraction. Finally, the **Power-Endurance** stage brings it all together: using as much muscle as efficiently as possible for as long as possible! These stages apply not only in the climbing specific exercises, but the weight training stages, and even the cardiovascular training (although the cardio stages have slightly different terminology) as well.

You may notice that a lot of the exercises are performed on a hangboard or bouldering wall. This was not intended to give an advantage to just the boulderers out there! Climbing walls are simply the most effective way to train for climbing specific muscle groups. Believe me, you will benefit from hitting the plastic as some of these exercises are almost impossible to do anywhere but the climbing gym. But if you are intent on only training for hand cracks, mountaineering routes, or ice, then don't worry. Just skip the fingerboard and bouldering exercises. I have added exercises that don't require the gym in every phase except the Hypertrophy Phase. You can substitute extra weight room Hypertrophy Phase time instead of the climbing specific exercises. Or be creative!

Grip Positions
Real climbing has an infinite type of holds to grab. However, they can be divided into six basic categories of ten positions. Trad climbers may notice that crack sizes aren't listed below and that shouldn't be a concern. Muscle gains for the holds below transfer the same to crack as they do face holds. To improve on crack climbing, follow the exercises just as you would if you were sport climbing. The holds listed work specific and different hand and forearm muscles. The ability to "jam" is a matter of technique, and should be practiced separately on your climbing days. The grip positions that are especially prone to finger injury are *starred* so don't overdo it on those! It is better to start on the *stared* positions before you become fatigued and more prone to injury.

Raining at Index, WA – Dry on the Playground Wall.
Eric Linthewaite Photo

Grip positions shown in order: Open Hand Grip, Sloper, Pinch: Wide and Narrow, Half-Pad Crimp*, Full Crimp With Thumb Lock, Two-Finger Pocket 2 Knuckles Deep*: Index and Middle Fingers, Pinky and Ring, Two-Finger Pocket 1 Knuckle Deep*: Index and Middle, Ring and Pinkie

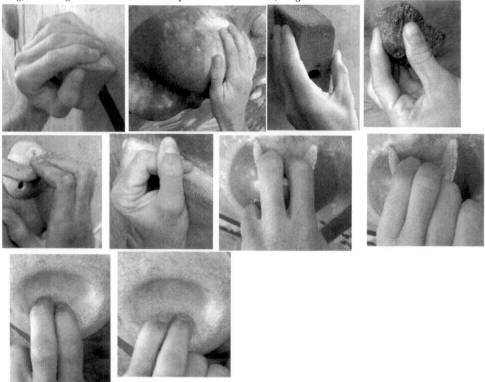

EXERCISES TO IMPROVE TECHNIQUE

Biofeedback

Having yourself videotaped is invaluable at any level. This will show you what your climbing partners were afraid to tell you, and provide insight into bad habits you may unknowingly have.

Velcro Gloves

This will help you save effort and improve your hand and footwork as well as route-finding skills. The rules state that once you touch a hold you cannot shift hand position on it. You're hand is "Velcro'd on". Place your foot exactly where you want it with no scraping, shifting, or any extra movement. You are allowed to pivot or change positions on the hold if the climb requires.

No Hands Climbing

Climb without using your hands to improve your footwork. You can only press the back of your hand into the wall.

Straight arm only climbing

Climbing with no bend in the elbows will force you to find better foot positions.

Dynamic as possible climbing

Experiment with pivoting your feet, back-stepping, drop-kneeing, lunging, and flagging on as many moves as possible to keep your climbing fluid and dynamic.

Open Feet
Use any feet on a problem over your limit. This will help you figure out how to climb on routes above your current level.

Add On
Make up a bouldering problem, with you and your partner adding a hold each move as you go. This will help you with route finding on harder problems.

Teach a beginner to climb
Teaching reinforces what you know and helps you to rationalize the information. You usually wind up teaching yourself.

Climb with someone who's better than you
This only works if they aren't so much better than you that you become frustrated. It also only works if you pay attention to the better climber!

Dry Tooling
Mixed climbers can practice dry tooling (climbing rock with crampons and ice tools) on homemade wooden holds, at the gym with plastic picks (ask the gym if it's ok), or outside on unpopular cliffs to become familiar with different grip positions on their ice tools, and to test the limit of what their tools can hold on to.

FOUNDATION CLIMBING EXERCISES
These exercises build technique experience, muscle endurance, and prime you to advance into the more difficult exercises.

General Climbing
One to two hours of leading or bouldering just below your grade. It should be something that you are "pumped" near the top, but aren't going to fall. Work one to two climbs just above your limit to stay sharp.

Uninterrupted Climbing
Two sets of 30-45 minutes sustained non-stop climbing or bouldering at one to three number grades below your level. Take 10 minute rest between sets. You should be breathing hard and "pumped", but *just* able to keep from falling.

HYPERTROPHY CLIMBING EXERCISES
You will need a hangboard or rock rings. You will also need a harness to clip weights onto, a weight belt, a weight vest, ankle and wrist weights, or a backpack and free weights. These exercises place a lot of stress on your fingers, shoulders, and elbows so pay attention to your body. Be sure to get adequate rest, and do a solid warm-up, cool-down, and stretch. Tape your fingers for the following exercises. The goal is to get those little muscles in your hand and forearm to fail, thus building strength and muscle fiber.

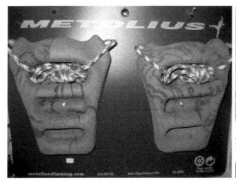 

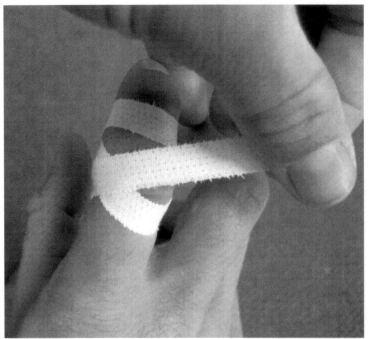

Tape to Prevent Injury

Beginning Hangboard, Rock Ring Workout - *Reps: 5 Sets: 6-10*
Perform five to ten second hangs using different grip positions. Take
five second rests between reps and two minute rests between sets. Do a
few 90 and 120 degree hangs in addition to doing straight arm hangs.
The main muscles you want to build are in your hand and forearm, so
the different hanging positions and arm degrees won't matter too much
(don't worry your biceps will be getting their work-out in the weight
training exercises in this stage). You will need to hang weight off the
harness or add weight another way so that you can barely do the last
rep of each set. Increase the weight each week.

Advanced Hangboard or Rock Ring Workout - *Reps: 6 Sets: 3*
Switch up the grips for either each rep, or each set. Take three second
rests between reps and three minute rests between sets. Add or subtract
weights to accomplish failure after each rep.

*Example: 1ˢᵗ rep: 7 second hang. 2ⁿᵈ rep: 6 second hang. 3ʳᵈ rep: 5
second hang. 4ᵗʰ rep 4 second hang. 5ᵗʰ rep: 3 second hang. 6ᵗʰ rep 2
second hang.*

Ice tool hangs: 180 Degree Hang, a 90 Degree Hang, and Staggered Hang
Ice climbers can add these in instead of using different grips. Straight arm, lock off, and staggered hangs are important now. Don't use leashes and if you have leashless tools, try gripping just above the ergo grips. If you don't want to use an ice tool you can easily use vertical dowel rods that are slightly wider than your tools. Drill a hole diagonally through the end and side of a foot long dowel rod wrapped in athletic tape, thread a knotted cord through the hole and tie a hook on the end of the cord. The point is that you want to make it more difficult than the real thing.

MAXIMUM RECRUITMENT CLIMBING EXERCISES

Plyometric muscle contractions are the most effective way to activate (or recruit) the most amount of muscle fibers involved in a specific movement. In climbing terms, this means doing exercises known as Dynos and "Campusing" will train your body to use more of the muscle you already have.

Campusing
Campusing is described as performing dynamic moves (dynos or deadpoints) on overhanging rungs at the limit of your reach – usually without the aid of your feet. Campusing is a great workout, but is the most dangerous for creating injuries. Heed all the warnings from all the different workouts, and stop if you even think you might be hurting yourself. Don't do more than two sessions per week and make sure you have three days rest in between. Tape your fingers and take two-three days rests before doing it again. Quit after you are no longer to explosively move between rungs to prevent injury.

Campusing Exercises - *Reps: 1-12. Sets:1-4. Rest between sets: 5-10 minutes*
Deadpoint
On a 45 degree wall or campus board do controlled one-arm lunges (feet on).
Single Dyno
Same as a deadpoint but with no feet (alternate arms).
Double Dyno
Both hands come (no feet) off to grab the next higher rung.
Drop Downs
Like a single dyno, but only *touch* the upper rung and then drop back down without actually grabbing the hold or rung. This is the most dangerous exercise. Limit your reps!

Deadpoint   Single Dyno   Double Dyno

No Feet Bouldering
Great for gyms without a campus board. Best performed on a 45 degree wall.

Speed Climbing
This is a much safer max recruitment exercise, although campusing will produce more pronounced gains in strength. Climb fifteen easy boulder problems or four easy routes as quickly and explosively as possible. Take 3-5 minute rests.

Rope or Ladder Climb
This is like campusing, but less climbing specific (although easier on the fingers). You will need a rope ladder (aka a Bachar Ladder) or make due with a fat gymnastics rope, a pegboard, a regular climbing rope, or and inverted ladder. Without using your feet, pull yourself up the rope.

Ice Climbing Specific Plyometrics
Try hooking the rungs of an inverted ladder or jungle-gym sans feet with your ice tools.

POWER ENDURANCE CLIMBING EXERCISES
This final stage of climbing-specific training brings the exercises together so you can develop both strength and endurance. Ice climbers can substitute dry tooling for most of the following exercises. One of the best ice climber training set-ups I've seen that incorporates power endurance involved laps of simply hooking bolt hangers attached to overhanging or completely inverted lengths of plywood.

Repetitive hold climbing, *Reps: 1-2. Sets: 6 (one of each grip positions). Rest 2 minutes.*
Like campusing, this is a very injury-prone exercise routine, but extremely effective. This exercise combines the static hangboard training with dynamic movement similar to laddering in the campusing exercises. You will need six of a similar hold for each hand, so unless you have tons of room or six hangboards, use H.I.T. strips by Nicros, or a similar product. Tape your fingers.

If you can do over 20 reps, add 5 pounds. Sit start to begin. Deadpoint up each hold of the same grip, drop back down, then up again until failure - while using any foothold you want.

Limit or Beyond Climbing: 4-5 laps total
Pick a few climbs at or above your limit which are about 100 moves or so long. Take 5-10 minute rests between routes. This can be done outside on a top rope.
Boulderers will have to choose a few more problems than roped climbers.

Weighted Climbing
Put enough weight in a backpack, weight vest, ankle/wrists weights, or attach weights to your harness so you can barely get up the route. Climb a few grades below your limit.

Progressive Bouldering
Climb fifteen problems in an easier to harder, back to easier fashion (aka pyramids) as fast as possible. The top of the pyramid is your hardest grade climbed yet. Climb 4 routes that are 3 grades below your limit, then climb two routes two grades below your limit. Next climb one route at one grade below your limit, followed by a route at your limit. Now climb back down the pyramid. Do one more route at a grade just below your limit, two more two grades below your limit, and finally four routes three grades below your limit.

Example: If the hardest route you've done so far is V5, then start by climbing four x V2s, two x V3s, one V4 and one V5. Go back down by doing one V4, two V3s, and last four V2s.

Repetitive Bouldering - *Sets: 4-8, Reps: 4-6. Rest: 2-4 minutes between sets*
Pick between four to six boulder problems (the reps) done back to back with no rest (one set). Rest 2-4 minutes and do it again – up to eight times. These should be mostly problems that you are familiar with but aren't easy. It's better to complete the problem than it is to fall off and start again.

Example: If you climb an occasional V3 and V4, do four to six V2's in a row, rest 2 to 4 minutes, then do it again three to eight more times with different problems at the same difficulty.

Drytool-Snowshoe-Bouldering
Pete Hirst Photo

WEIGHT TRAINING

If you only climbed, or just did the climbing specific exercises, there would be quite a bit of muscle imbalances in your body. Hitting the weight room not only rounds out your routine, but helps to prevent injury by strengthening muscles that don't get used and abused by climbing. Also, the weight room allows you to develop the larger muscles used in climbing much more rapidly and effectively than climbing specific training could accomplish.

Most of these exercises only require dumbbells and a pull-up bar (ice tools, dowel rods, and rock rings are great substitutes for the pull-up bar). Tubing, cable machines, Swiss balls (inflatable exercise balls), and barbells are optional. Form is absolutely crucial, as is a spotter for heavy lifting. General form advice includes: bending at the waist, keeping your elbows in, shoulders down, neck neutral, and knees slightly bent.

Two to three days of recovery is necessary before repeating hypertrophy, maximum recruitment, or power endurance exercises. Don't do every exercise for an area in one work-out: alternate exercises. Pay attention to form and remember to breathe. Unguarded movements are what cause injury. There are too many exercises listed to possibly do in a week, so try and alternate the exercises. Focus on the weak areas first, and pick up the rest of the exercises later in the workout. The point of the exercise is in *doing* the exercise, not getting it over with. So remember to lift and lower the weights slowly and controlled. Ten slow, controlled pull-ups are more effective for climbing than 40 quick frantic pull-ups. Climbing is a slow, controlled sport. The training for quick bursts of motion like dynoing is covered in the climbing-specific section of the manual.

A warm-up, cool-down, and stretch are necessary to recover and prevent injury. Do not over-train the shoulder abductors or external rotators, and do not do any military presses (explained later). Your total time in the weight room should be about one to two hours if you did a good job warming up, cooling down, stretching, and did not climb that day. If you combine the strength workout with a climbing workout, then focus on the muscles that didn't get fatigued during your climbing routine.

By no means are these exercises all-inclusive! I've chosen the most specific climbing exercises and supplemented specific exercises that work the commonly injured underused muscles. I've included as many photos as possible, including some pretty advanced exercises. Imagination is the only limitation as to what exercises you can do! I have specific regional exercise routines that are, in general, far more exhaustive than the sport specific ones outlined below … otherwise you'd never be able to leave the gym!

To find out how much weight to use, first find out the maximum weight you can lift one time, and one time only (your max). Multiply your max by the percentages given to find out how much weight to lift . For core and general strength routines, take some time and find out how much weight it takes to get a muscle burn or shaking within the number reps given.

Below are the phases of weight training, just like the different climbing phases. The core routines aren't actually a "phase", but you will be gaining strength and endurance as you add reps and more difficult exercises. This is not a complete book on all the different exercises you can do. There are literally thousands of exercises and stretches out there for the purpose of weight training, injury rehab, and other sports. I've added helpful rehab exercises in the injury section. The following are just the ones helpful in climbing.

A Note on Cross Fit
Cross-fit and similar exercises programs are becoming extremely popular with climbers and rightly so. However, I have not included specific Cross-Fit exercises since Cross-Fit programs and exercises are vast and varied. A major problem with some of these programs is how easy it is to get injured! I highly recommend that you attain an excellent base level of conditioning before participating in these activities (at least two months of regular weight training and cardio). If you are interested in cross-fit or similar exercise programs, please explore them and take advantage of the great benefits that you can gain. My advice to adding a cross-fit similar exercise program to this one would be to not skip on any of the actual climbing parts of this program and skip as little of the cardio as possible. Swap out any of the General Weight sessions, and just one of the Hypertrophy, Max-Recruitment, or Power-Endurance per week.

GENERAL STRENGTH

Sets: 2-3. Reps: 8-15. Weight: (Use enough weight so that the last rep is very challenging, but you still could pull off a couple more).

If you are new to this or it's been a while, you may have to experiment and take time to find the right weight for you. These are your general fitness exercises to build a baseline of strength and to prepare your tendons and ligaments for the more difficult exercises.

HYPERTROPHY

Sets: 6-10. Reps: 4-6. Weight: Lift 80-85% of your max
Train only three to four muscle groups per workout. Do a few medium weight reps of the same exercise before you begin to warm-up and excite the muscle. Rest two to three days before you do the same exercise again. If you don't fail by the last rep, you need to add more weight. This is how you build more muscle and get stronger!

Hypertrophy Exercises: Pull-ups or Lat Pulls, Biceps curl, Bench press, Rows, Finger curls, Step-ups or One-legged squats, Squats or Leg press, and Hamstring curls. Optional exercises: Calf raises and Hammer swings.

Example: Bench Press. If your max is 150 pounds, then do 8 or so reps around 60 pounds to warm up. Then you will lift around 125 pounds 4 to 6 times, rest, and do it 5 to 9 more times. Do another hypertrophy exercise that works another muscle group like finger curls and squats instead of something like pull-ups that works almost the same muscles.

MAXIMUM RECRUITMENT

Sets: 6-10. Reps: 1-3. Weight: Lift 90-100% of your max
Exercise three to four muscle groups per workout at the most. Do a few medium weight reps of the same exercise before you begin to warm-up and excite the muscle. Rest two to three days before doing the same exercise again. If you don't fail by the last rep, add more weight. These exercises train you to use the muscle you've built!

Maximum Recruitment Exercises: Pull-ups or Lat Pulls, Biceps Curls, Bench Press, Rows, Finger Curls, and Squats or Leg Presses.

Example: Bench Press if your max is 150 pounds. Warm up with around 8 reps at 60 pounds or so. Now bench around 140 pounds 1 to 3 times and rest. Do it 5 to 9 more times.

POWER-ENDURANCE

6 reps to failure at 80-85% max, then 1 rep at 100% max (failure)
Add two to five pounds for the 6-rep phase after each set. Work three to four muscle groups at most per workout. Do a few medium weight reps before you begin to warm-up and excite the muscle. Rest two to three days. These exercises train you to use the muscles you've built for extended periods of time as efficiently as possible, but require that you've completed the previous stages. To mix it up you can do a similar-type exercise used in the hypertrophy phase, but not in the Max Recruit phase for the 6-rep part of these exercises.

Power-Endurance Exercises: Pull-ups or Lat Pull, Biceps Curls, Bench Press, Rows, Finger Curls, and Squats or Leg Press –the same exercises as Max Recruitment.

Example: Bench Press (if max = 150 pounds). Do about 8 reps of 60 pounds to warm up. Lift around 125 pounds six times then lift 150 pounds once. Now lift 130 pounds six times, then 150 pounds. Finally lift 135 pounds six times then 150 pounds once.

UPPER BODY EXERCISES

The exercises shown below are the major prime movers for climbing. *starred* exercises are also used in the hypertrophy, max recruitment, and/or power-endurance routines. For all exercises keep your head neutral, shoulders down, feet in a fencer's stance, pelvis neutral, and abs engaged unless the exercise specifically will not allow for this posture.

Pull-ups*
Have your palms foreword and hands shoulder width apart. You can substitute rock-rings, ice tools, or vertical dowel rods to simulate your type of climbing for all the pull up exercises. Rock rings or vertical dowel rods are the best for your elbows since they allow you to rotate your arms. Use a cable lat pull machine if you are unable to add weight, or for strength training with a high amount of weight. Avoid leading with your head and jutting your chin. Pull-up all the way to a lock-off, and lower down just before your elbows lock out.

Alternate Pull-Up exercises. To mix it up, try substituting some of these for the good old fashioned pull up:

Negative Pull-ups
Slowly lower down from a lock off. Be careful, if overdone this can cause injury.

Staggered Pull-ups
One hand is higher than other. Use a towel if you don't have rock rings, dowel rods, or ice tools.

Lock-offs
Isometric hold at various arm angles (45, 90, 135 degrees). Hold until failure (so do these later in the workout!)

Dynamic Pull-ups
Use a pull-up bar, rock-rings, or ice-tools. Pull-up and lock off for 5 seconds at the top of the pull-up. Lower down, pull-up again, then lower down to 90 degree lock-off for 5 seconds. Lower down, pull-up, and lower down to 120 degree lock-off for 5 seconds, and finally lower.

| Pull-Ups | Staggered Pull-Ups | Lock-Offs |

Lat Pull-downs*
Essentially works the same muscle groups as a pull-up, but less sport specific. The advantage is it that this is much easier and safer to use if you are pulling very heavy loads. The bar goes in front of your head, not behind to avoid shoulder and neck injury.

Biceps curl*

Use dumbbells. Keep your elbows tucked, and shoulders down. Lower just until your arm is locked. Do not use momentum to make it easier.

Push-ups

Use your fists if you are experiencing wrist problems. Add challenge by using your feet on a Swiss ball, hands on push-up bars, or try it one handed.

Bench press*

Use dumbbells unless you can press so much you need a barbell. Get a spotter with the barbell. Uses similar muscle groups as a push-up, but less sport-specific. The advantage is it is easier to add weight.

Rows*

Can be done via a standing cable machine, seated cable machine, or bent-over with a dumbbell. Focus on keeping your scapula down and in. The motion comes from your lats, and finishes the range of motion with your rhomboids.

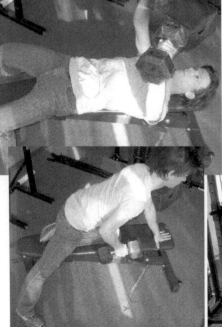

Triceps curl

You can use a standing cable rope grip machine, parallel bars, supine with dumbbells, or with body weight on a bench (feet elevated on a Swiss ball for challenge).

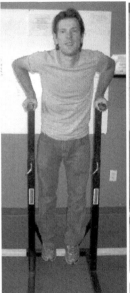

One arm pull down

You can use a standing cable rope grip machine or rubber tubing. Like a standing triceps cable curl, but start above your head and follow through behind your back.

Hammer swing*

Attach a cable machine or rubber tubing behind you - or add head weights to your ice tool. Pretend like you are swinging an ice-tool. This exercise can be used in the hypertrophy phase for ice-climbers.

Finger Curls*
This is a Hypertrophy and Power Endurance stage specific exercise. Curl a barbell with your fingers, not your wrists. Keep arms straight and elbows tucked in. Use equal to or more than your body weight if finding you max is hard.

Wrist Curls
You can go into a wrist curl from the above exercise, or you can just use dumbbells instead of a big barbell for the general strength phase. You really only need to do this exercise if you're not doing much else in the way of forearm training.

Weighted Dowel Roll
Attach a weight to a dowel rod with some cord, and curl the weight up, then turn your palms down to slowly lower it. Essentially combines wrist curls and reverse wrist curls in one exercise.

Farmer's Carry
Pinch grip something heavy and wide (like a phone book or a Olympic weight) and carry it around with you until you drop it. A good "at work" exercise.

40

LOWER BODY EXERCISES

These exercises are mainly for alpinists, or for sport climbers who are also runners, bicyclists, etc. Squats (including Step-Ups) and Leg Presses are the only ones used in the hypertrophy, max recruitment, and power-endurance routines due to the high probability of injury if you were to do lunges or step-ups with heavy weights (calf raises optional). *Starred* exercises should receive the most focus. The different lunge and squatting exercises can all be swapped out. Two sets of two lunge or squat exercises make a good functional lower body workout.

> **Note on Lunges and Squats**: Keep your feet evenly spaced and pointed straight ahead. Keep your back straight, and your abs engaged. Your front knee is not to go beyond your ankle joint. For squats, initiate the motion with your butt by sticking it out behind you. Control your descent. One-leg squats need to be slow and controlled.

Squats*
You can use a barbell or dumbbells depending on how much weight you need.

One Leg Squats*
Use just your body weight, or use dumbbells on the side opposite the leg you are working. On the ground, flag the other foot behind you, or stand on a bench to clear your leg. Lower down as far as you can get back up without using your hands on your thighs to help.

Step-ups*
Use body weight or dumbbells. Step up on bench so if bottom foot is on ground, then the height of bench should have your upper leg bent at 90 degrees at the hip and knee respectively.

| One Leg Squat | Step-Ups | Sideways Step-Up |

Leg press machine*

A supine leg press machine is necessary for very heavy loads. Squats are far better, but if you don't have a spotter, then this is a safer bet. Try squeezing a ball between your knees to add more functional training to the exercise.

Wall Squats

Squeeze a medicine ball between your legs to work your inner thighs. You can use a Swiss ball behind your back to make it easier. Perform isometric holds at 90 degrees or more. Feel the burn!

Lunges

With dumbbells or body weight. Lunge up and down the room, dumbbells in both hands.

Dynamic Lunges

Skip in place, stair hop, and skip side to side with or without weight.

Calf raises*
Barbell or machine. You can add this to the hypertrophy or power endurance stages if you have weaker than average calves. Some lucky folks with Popeye legs can skip this exercise altogether.

Hamstring Curl*
Use a machine unless your hamstrings are especially weak – then use tubing.

****

CORE TRAINING

Your abs get all the press when it comes to talking about your "core". In reality, every body part has smaller postural muscles that can become over-fatigued due to lack of training, or just as commonly, become overwhelmed when much larger muscle groups become overdeveloped. Think of these exercises as strengthening the "weak link" in the chain. If you are weak in a certain area, or are recovering from injury, then work the other muscle groups for that area (unless there is pain!). Refer to the injury section for specific recommendations. These exercises train the non-climbing specific muscles and can be done daily.

I've included what's called **Lumbar Stability Tracks**. Each track patterns after an archetypal functional movement pattern with emphasis on particular lumbar core stabilizers. Go through the tracks to see where it starts to get difficult and start the progression there. You can do multiple exercises from each track and work your way to the advanced exercises. Keep your pelvis "neutral" (not rocked too far forward or backward) throughout exercises unless the exercise says otherwise, and have your core remain perfectly still. If there is wobbling, shaking, or loss of form within the first few seconds, you are not ready for the exercise.

Do at least two sets of each of the following muscle groups per core workout: Abs (including Obliques), Back Extensors, Gluts, Leg Abductors, Hip Flexors, Shoulder Stabilizers, Wrist Extensors, and Neck Stabilizers.

> *Example: A well rounded core routine would be: 2 sets of 25 glut pumps each leg, 20 oblique curl-ups, 1 set of 100's, 2 sets of 15 back-ups, 2 sets of 15 side leg lifts, 2 sets of 12 leg lifts on prone bridge with a ball, 2 minutes each of prone plank, and side plank (both sides), 2 sets of reverse dips, 2 sets serratus punches and reverse wrist curls 20 lbs each side, and finally 2 sets of 15 neck retractions.*

Most of these exercises can be done daily and are not done with heavy weights or to failure. They make a great addition to the end of any workout.

Perform 2-3 sets of 15-50 reps, or a 1-2 minute hold depending on the exercises.
Muscle burn is your goal, but stop the exercise when excessive shaking occurs. Since there are so many exercises listed, skip the ones you don't have a problem with. Focus on the exercises you shake on or have bit of difficulty with and progress from there. Exercises that you want to do frequently are *starred*.

NECK STABILIZERS
Chin Retraction*
Pull your chin in without flexing your neck as if making a double chin. Hold for 3 seconds, and repeat. To strengthen further, put a pillow or Nerf ball behind your head against the wall and squeeze. To add balance, try adding correct breathing with pelvic tilts, while performing wall or ground angels all at the same time. This is an excellent functional full body integration rehab exercise.

Isometric Deep Neck Flexion
Keep your head hovering just above the ground when lying on your back. Hold until shaking occurs. Keep your chin tucked in as in the chin retraction exercise.

WRIST STABILIZERS

Reverse Wrist Curls*
Use a dumbbell or tubing. Support your wrist and do not hyperextend.

Finger extension with rubber bands
Find a rubber band that fits around all your fingers and thumb. Open up your hand, splaying your fingers. Try with different thicknesses of rubber bands. Also you can loop the rubber band around different fingers and spread them apart individually.

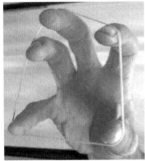

Supination and Pronation
Hold a dumbbell with weight in one fist. Turn your palm up and down. You can also use tubing.

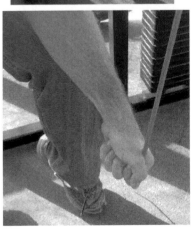

Radial and Ulnar Deviation
Hold a dumbbell in your hand and rotate your wrist up and down toward your thumb and pinky. You can use tubing for ulnar deviation.

45

SHOULDER STABILIZERS

Reverse Dips

Between two chairs or parallel bars, support your body off the ground with your arms fully extended. Now push your body up using your lower traps and serratus.

Serratus Punch*
Use a cable machine or tubing while standing, or supine with a dumbbell. Hold your arm out in front of your body with your elbow fully extended. Now slowly "punch" your arm forward without rotating your body. Only a few inches of movement need to occur. Your elbow is locked throughout the exercise.

Push-Up Plus on Ball
With your body in a prone plank position and both feet on a stability ball, do a push-up. At the end of the push-up finish with an extra "punch" as in the above exercise.

Wide-Grip Lat Pull Downs*
With your arms spread past shoulder width apart, only pull the bar down until your shoulder blades come fully down and in. All movement comes from the shoulder blades, not the shoulders.

Wall or Ground Angels*
Using your shoulder blades (not your shoulders) perform an angel (like a snow angel) against the wall or on the floor. To do this, pull your shoulder blades in and down. Remember, all the movement should be initiated by your shoulder blades, not your arms or shoulders.

Prone Shoulder Flexion
Begin lying face down on a weight bench with your arm hanging down towards the floor while holding a light amount of weight (0-10 lbs). Raise your straightened arm up past shoulder level as if holding a torch, keeping your thumb up. Stop if your shoulder hurts, pops, or grinds.

47

Sword and Seatbelt*

Using tubing or an adjustable cable machine, pretend you are unsheathing a sword as you raise your arm diagonally up and across your body. To "sheath" the sword, the cable or tubing must be above your head. For the seatbelt, have your hand by your opposite shoulder and bring it down to your opposite hip like you are putting on a seatbelt. To "undo" the seatbelt, the cable or tubing needs to be below your arm. For both exercises, it is extremely important that you keep your shoulders down.

Sword

Sheathing the Sword

Seatbelt

Taking the Seatbelt Off

Gorilla Pull
With heavy tubing or cable, pull both arms straight back using only your lats and rhomboids. This is a good exercise to add to a workout every once in a while.

****

LUMBAR CORE STABILIZERS

Remember to **keep the non-moving parts of your body as still as possible**. Exercises with simple motions are meant to be repeated multiple times, usually alternating limbs. Hold static (isometric) positions until shaking occurs. Most exercises seem easy until you do them 20-30 times. Move to the next harder exercise when you can do it perfectly. It is very important to get good at the first few exercises in each track.

Pelvic Tilt Track (Abs, Back Extensors)

1. Neutral Pelvis and Clocking

With your back straight, roll your pelvis forward then backward on a ball or disc. Imagine your pelvis like tipping a bowl back and forth with your abs. Next, go side to side, in a circle, then a fig-8.

2. Pelvic Tilts Supine

Begin lying on your back with knees bent, feet flat on the floor, and arms on your stomach. Slowly rock your pelvis backward (a posterior pelvic tilt) in order to press the small of your back into the ground. Hold for a couple seconds. Your lips should be pursed and breathing out while actively flattening your stomach. It should be a forceful, sustained push with your low back and abs. If there was a foam ball under your back you would be crushing it. Now slowly rock your pelvis forward and allow your back to slightly arch. Breathe in and expand your stomach. Repeat 15-20 times.

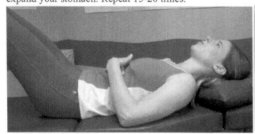

3. Pelvic Tilts on a Ball

The motion is exactly the same as supine, but done sitting on a gym ball. The gym ball adds extra resistance, but the exercise is more difficult. The ball should not roll back and forth at all. Instead, as you tuck your tailbone into the ball, the ball should flatten slightly.

Supine Track (Abs, Hip Flexors)

1. Single Leg Raise.

Raise one leg up and down, keeping your abs engaged and body still.

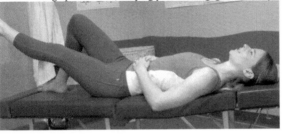

2. Alternate Arm and Leg Raise.

Raise opposite arm and leg, switch sides, and repeat.

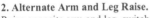

3. Unstable Leg Raise

Using a foam roller hold a medicine ball and do bent knee raises, marching in place.

4. Unstable Alternate Arm and Leg Raise

Using a foam roller and a medicine ball under your head, do alternate leg and arm lifts.

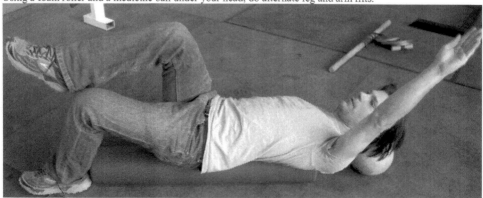

5. Swiss Ball Leg Lifts

Holding a Swiss ball between your legs and off the floor while doing alternate arm lifts.

Quadruped Track (Back Extensors, Gluts)

1. Single Arm Raise.

Raise one arm, lower, switch arms, and repeat.

2. Single Leg Raise
Same as the above exercise.

3. Alternate Arm and Leg Raise
Raise alternate arm and leg, switch sides, and repeat.

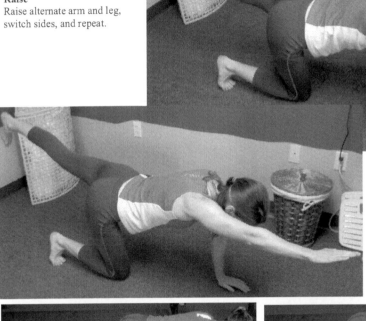

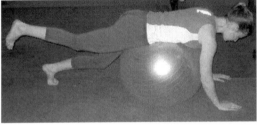

4. Knee Push on a Ball
The key is to actively push your knee into the ball to activate the hip flexors.

5. Quadruped on a Ball
Perform single arm and leg raises, then alternate both arm and leg at the same time.

53

6. Quadruped on a Wobble Board

7. Quadruped with Arms Together

8. Quadruped with Torso Dips
Rotate your torso to the floor and back up.

9. Quadruped on Foam Rollers

Prone Track (Gluts, Back Extensors)

1. Gluteal Squeeze
Lying face-down, actively squeeze your buttocks to activate them (not shown).

2. Single Arm and Leg Raise
Raise one arm, then one leg laying face down, similar to the quadruped track (not shown).

3. Dual Arm and Leg Raise
Raise both arms, then both legs.

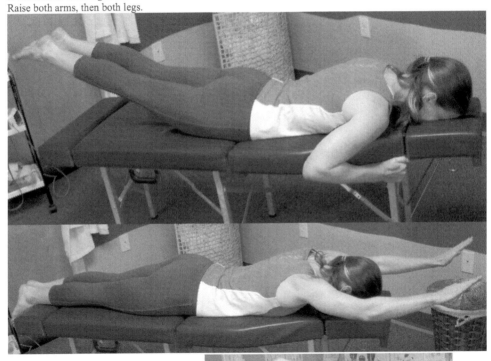

4. Gluteal Pumps
Pump toward the ceiling with a bent knee.

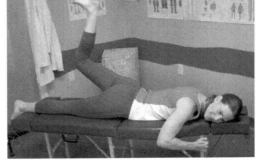

5. Alternate Arm and Leg Raise
Raise alternate arms and leg at the same time similar to the quadruped track (not shown).

6. Torso Raises
On a bench or sit-up table, do torso raises.

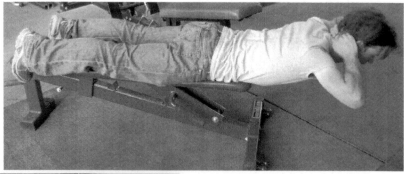

7. Leg Curls
Using a bench, do leg curls and raises.

8. Glut Pumps on a Ball

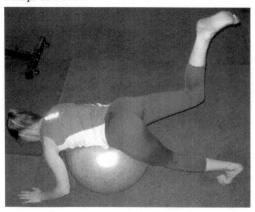

56

9. Torso Raises on a Ball

10. Double Leg Raise on a Ball

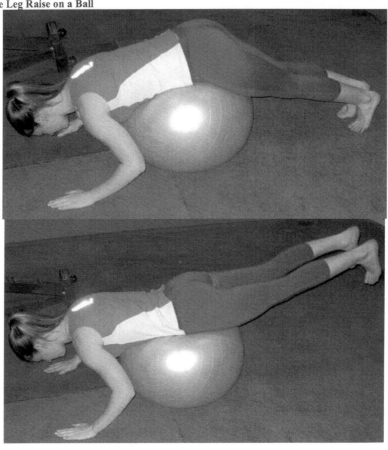

11. Superman
Hold statically as long as possible.

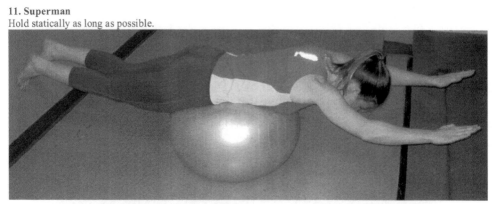

12. Hip flexion on a Ball

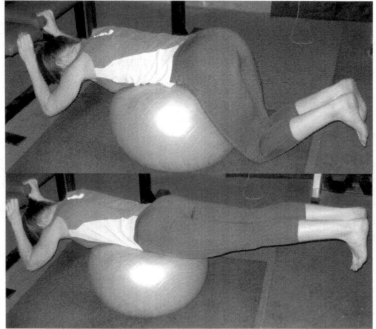

Bridge Track (Abs, Gluts, Adductors, Abductors, Hip Flexors)

1. The Bridge

You can drop your buttocks up and down for reps, or hold the position isometrically.

2. Heel Lift

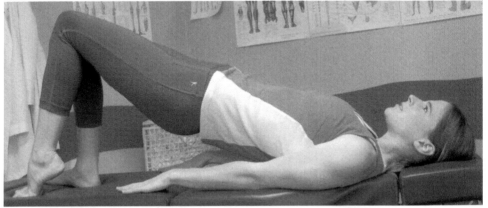

3. Bent Knee Lift

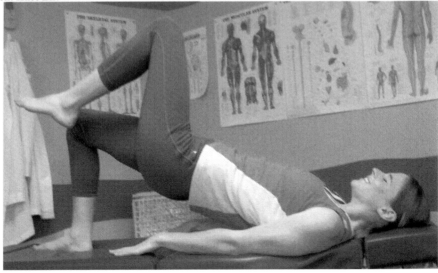

4. Leg Lift
Try this with your arms hovering just above the floor.

5. Leg Raise and Lower

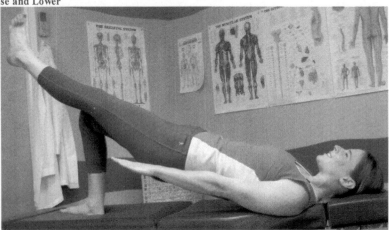

6. Ball Squeeze. Perform a bridge while squeezing a ball or pulling a resistance band open.

7. Resistance Band or Tubing

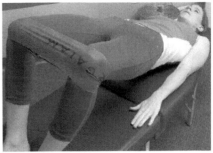

8. Unstable Bridge

Get in the bridge position on a ball, but do dips by dropping your buttocks down and up while keeping your torso and feet steady.

The next photos are just like the heel lift and leg raise/lower but with a ball for instability

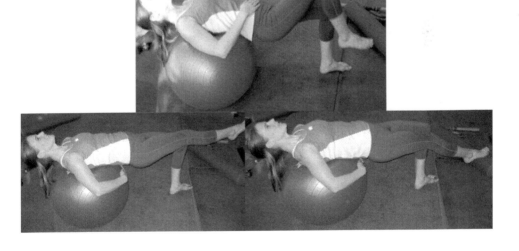

9. Reverse Bridge on Ball. Raise and lower your buttocks. Try keeping your arms off the floor.

10. Reverse Bridge with Straight Leg Lifts on Ball. Try this without the support of your arms on the floor.

11. Reverse Bridge Hamstring Curls

Side-Bridge Track (Adductors, Back Extensors, Abs)
1. Side Bridge with Isometric Hold.

2. Side Dips
Start as in the above photo (#1), and dip your hips down and up.

3. Leg and Arm Raise. Hold statically.

4. Torso raise
Have someone hold your feet or find some way to keep them down.

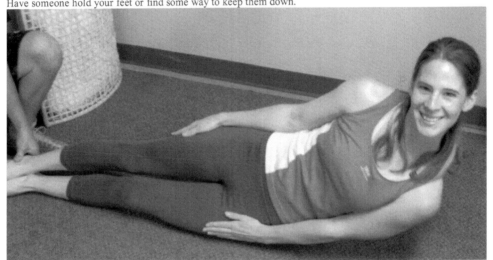

Side-Lying Track (Adductors, Abductors, Hip Flexors, Gluts)

1. Clamshell
Open and close your thighs. Try with lower legs elevated (shown) or on the ground.

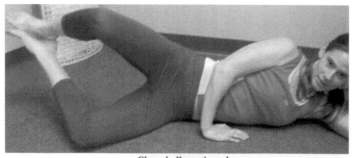

...Clamshell continued

2. Leg Raise
Raise and lower your upper leg with your foot pointed slightly down.

3. Double Leg Raise
Raise and lower both legs

4. Lower Leg Raise
Cross your upper leg over your lower. Raise your lower leg up and down.

5. Upper Leg Lowers
Point your foot and toes towards the floor and do small, short, quick leg raises.

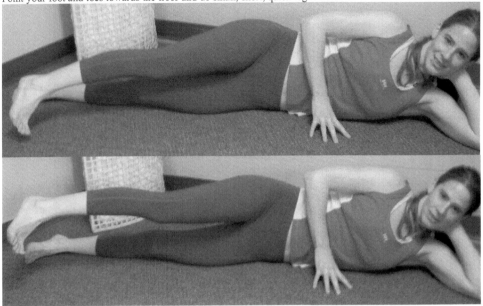

6. Leg Circles
Point your foot and toes slightly down. Extend your leg in front and perform large and small leg circles in both directions.

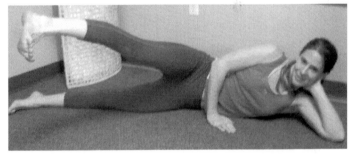

7. Standing Hip Drops
Standing on one leg, drop your opposite hip and raise it back up without using momentum, your upper body, or your leg. The motion comes from your hip joint only. You can use a ball on the side you're standing on for support. This exercise is technically not on your "side" but it works muscles similar to the others in this track.

65

Abdominal Track (Abs, Hip Flexors)

1. Prone Plank

With your body in a rigid prone plank position, perfectly straight, prop yourself up on both elbows shoulder width apart and hold for time. Stop when shaking occurs.

Plank shown on a wobble disc for added difficulty

2. Reverse Crunch

On your back, flex your hips and knees into a 90/90 degree position. Place your hands at your sides. You may use your arms to help, but as you progress try only to use your abs. To begin, lift your hips and low back off the ground slowly, and return to the ground slowly. The moment your hips touch the ground again, straighten your legs and lower them slowly to just off the ground, and slowly return them to the original 90/90 position.

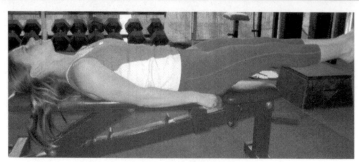

3. Crunches

On a ball or the floor, gently support the back of your head without interlocking your fingers. Do not pull on your head, but instead try and lightly rest your head in your hands to avoid neck strain. Press your low back into the ground first and hold it there. Now, using only your abs, lift your torso up until the bottom of your shoulder blades are off the ground or ball. Slowly lower back down. The more controlled and slowly you perform this, or any exercise, the more effective it will be. One slow and controlled good rep is worth a thousand quick reps with poor form.

4. Oblique Crunches

With shoulder blades off table and head neutral, turn your torso towards the opposite raised knee. Can be done on a ball.

5. "100's"

Keeping a neutral pelvis and neck, raise your upper back off the matt until your shoulder blades are off the matt. Now lift both legs (hovering just off the ground is the most difficult) and hold them there. Pump both arms simultaneously one hundred times!

6. Hanging Sit-ups

Lock-off arms at 90 degrees on a pull-up bar, rock-rings, ice-tools, or dowel rods. Raise both knees towards your chest and back down to 90 degrees. Turn your knees and crunch to opposite shoulders and back down to 90 degrees to work the obliques.

7. Wood Chop

Flex your trunk forward using a cable or tubing.

8. Weighted Sit-ups

Sitting on a ball and holding a weight, do sit ups.

9. Reverse sit-up on a ball

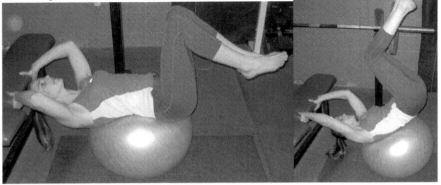

EXERCISE TO AVOID OR LIMIT

The following exercises are not recommended or should be done sparingly with light weight. They place excessive strain on your rotator cuff, wrists, or knees, and can result in injury.

Military (Overhead) Press
This popular exercise combines the two of most dangerous positions for your shoulders: abduction and external rotation - and loads them in these positions (see the injury section for more details as to why).

Arm Abduction (Side Lifts)
These are really only necessary for shoulder rehab since they place your shoulder in a dangerous position (see the injury section for more details as to why). If you're going to do these, just use light weight in a pain free range of motion.

Internal and External Rotation
Once again, these exercises are really only necessary for shoulder rehab. If you're going to do these, just use light weight in a pain-free range of motion. Unless you've just had surgery, your internal rotators will be worked plenty in other exercises, and the external rotators are small and extremely injury prone.

Weighted Shoulder Shrugs
Your upper traps are very strong - unless you've been seriously injured. See the correct version of how to do a shoulder shrug in the core section.

Quad Extension on a Machine
This places un-physiologic stresses on your knees (in other words it grinds up your knees and excessively loads your ligaments). Squats and lunges are much better exercises for your knees.

Handheld Finger Trainers
Gripmasters, gyroscopic balls, or other finger and wrist devices are not recommended if you are doing the other finger training detailed above. Overuse injuries may occur.

Neck Circles and Neck Rotation Stretches
Both of these are unsafe for your neck and are not included. The joints in your neck are irritated by full neck circles (listen to the clicking and grinding), and it is much to easy to strain your neck by rotating it too far.

CARDIOVASCULAR TRAINING

Great cardiovascular fitness is a benefit to anyone in any sport. If you are a plateauing sport climber, maybe this is your weak link. Alpinists can directly benefit from cardio training for moving fast on approaches and on climbs.

There are many ways to get your heart rate up, but it's a good idea to find an activity that you can control your heart rate at will. Pick what you enjoy. Outside this may include running, biking, running stairs or hills, or cross-country skiing. Inside this may include a treadmill, Stairmaster, versa-climber, elliptical, stationary bike, a rowing machine, or swimming.

Be acutely aware of how your body is doing, as injury can strike easily to someone in an intense cardio program - which is what this is. Being able to move fast and strong in the mountains is just as crucial to being able to climb hard, so an alpinist's workout is going to be twice as hard. No one ever said mountain climbing was easy! But it's also important for all climbers to have a good cardiovascular fitness. Anyone who's climbed a long pitch at their limit knows that it feels like they are running a marathon.

If you start to feel pain, STOP, and re-evaluate. Since technique is crucial in activities like running, you may just need to try a lower impact type of cardio. Talk to a doctor before you begin the aerobic or anaerobic threshold training if you have any concerns.

A heart rate monitor is crucial to at least get started finding your zones. Cardio workouts are generally better after climbing or weight training for the hypertrophy stages, but during maximum recruitment and power-endurance stages it is best to do your cardio before the work-out. You can geek out on this as there are volumes written on this subject. It doesn't matter what your VO2 max is, and many climbers who would only run if chased leave highly trained runners in the dust on the approach.

Max Heart Rate (Max HR)

Multiply your Max HR by the percentages given to find your target heart rate and the intensity you need to keep that rate. To find your Max HR, either go all out with a heart rate monitor – or use the following equation.

Max HR = 208 - (0.7 * age)

Example for a 31 year old: .7x31 = 21.7 Round up or down unless you're obsessive. 208 - 22= 186 beats per minute = max heart rate. Note: A 31 year old's heart rate could go well above 186bpm, so the term Max HR is just semantics.

Below are the three major types of cardio training:

MODERATE AEROBIC

70-80% of your MaxHR. 45min-2hour sessions

This is the foundation. Go jogging on moderate terrain, a long uphill hike with your pack on, moderate spinning, elliptical, Stairmaster, rowing machine, or cross-country skiing: any activity you can sustain for 45 min to 2 hours at 70-80% MaxHR. This is your average trail run or steep approach with a heavy pack. These exercises will build your general endurance. Approaches to climbs can double up your cardio and climbing days!

AEROBIC THRESHOLD
One to two sets of 80 to 90% of your MaxHR for one 12-25 min rep.
You need one to two days rest before doing this exercise again. Good exercises are: a hard spin cycle, Stairmaster with a pack on, and uphill jogging. Be sure to warm-up and cool-down. This will build your ability to maintain a fast pace for longer periods of time. This is like the hypertrophy stage in the climbing and weight programs. Basically, find a big old hill that takes 30-45 minutes to run up with a break in the middle. Be sure and walk or at least go easy getting back down.

ANAEROBIC THRESHOLD
All Out 100% Max HR. Five 15-60sec bursts with 5 min rests between bursts. **You NEED 2-3 day rests before doing this exercise again.**
Uphill sprints, or a treadmill that is maxed out on the angle and speed (without falling off of it) are good examples. Be sure to warm-up and cool-down.
This exercise trains you to buffer lactic acid in your bloodstream more efficiently – an important ability for all types of climbing. This stage is similar to the maximum recruitment stages.

There is no "power endurance" stage for the cardio training. Instead, the Aerobic and Anaerobic Threshold stages are done on alternating days during the power endurance phase of the program.

A note on running technique:
Running is one of the few sports where we were never taught proper technique. No wonder so many runners get injured. Humans were designed to run, but I guess once we became more sedentary and encased our feet in footwear, we somehow lost the basic skill-set. Check out "Chi Running" and "Pose Running" techniques to see if they help your form. Heel to toe running is how most folks run, even though a mid foot or toe strike is a softer and safer form of running. Also, more natural footwear is out there (although barefoot would be ideal after much training) such as the Vibram 5-Finger "shoe". Crocs, Chuck Taylors, and Sandals are biomechanically sounder than most high-tech running shoes. No-no's include tapered and upturned toes, and elevated heels.

****

STRETCHING

Why is this section last in the chapter!? Your main stretching session should happen after the work-out. Your warm-up should accomplish loosening up your muscles. If a particular muscle group is outrageously stiff, then go ahead and stretch it lightly after a solid warm-up, but don't work that area hard at the beginning of your focused workout. Then stretch that area morning noon and night! This advice to stretch only after exercise may come as a major threat to some folks who have it imbedded in their psyche that the stretching should come first. This does not mean you shouldn't warm up! Light cardio and moving your limbs through their full range of motion is an essential activity to prevent injury and perform well.

Most tight muscles aren't tight because they are shortened, but because your nervous system is causing them to constantly over-contract. Warming up helps to have your nervous system "let go" of the muscle, along with increased blood flow and warmth. Now your muscles are at a perfect balance of loose and taught - ready for action, and any stretching beyond this point will only help for long-term gains in muscle length, not to aid in performance. Stretching a muscle resets its kinesthetic information (its ability to know where it is in space) so the possibility of injury is actually *higher* if you stretch before a work-out or climb. Also, stretching a muscle that isn't completely warmed up can cause micro-tears. Think of your muscles as a leather belt and your nervous system as the buckle. Sure, you can stretch the belt out when it's buckled, but it would be a lot more effective and efficient to first undo the buckle?

After the work-out or climb, your muscles should now be as loose as they are going to get. This is the best time to do a long sustained stretch. To get a good stretch, ease into the stretch to meet the resistance barrier. Do not force your muscles past this point. **Hold the stretch for 20-45 seconds while gently increasing the stretch.** Start with the stiffest muscles on the stiffest side first to ensure you give them their full attention. A stretching session should last about 15-20 minutes. A rest day should involve a good full body stretching session (or take a yoga class).

Advanced Stretching

This stretching technique builds on the theory that your muscles are ultimately controlled by your nervous system. Muscle Energy Technique (MET) effectively "resets" the resting tone of a muscle and attempts to keep it there. This technique requires an active contraction with a stretch. You can get the best results with a partner.
Initiation: Contract the muscle you want to stretch at 100% for 10 seconds then fully relax.
Step 1: Bring the limb actively to its new resistance barrier, and initiate a full stretch for 10 seconds.
Step 2: Without moving out of the stretch, contract that muscle at 100% for 5-7 seconds.
Repeat step 1 and 2 twice more.
Step 3 (partner required): Have your partner push your limb in the opposite direction you were stretching it so you are just barely able to overcome his or her resistance - back to a resting position.

The hamstring (below), psoas, piriformis, tensor fascia latea, adductors, quadratus lumborum, and erector spinae muscles are great candidates for this type of stretching. The upper body is more difficult and also more prone to injury from overstretching to use this technique on. Self –M.E.T. can be effectively done with any stretch – just stretch as normal, then press against the stretch, and see if you can stretch farther.

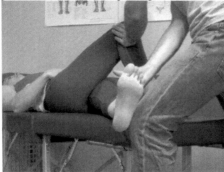 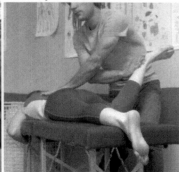

Stretching the left TFL   Stretching the Piriformis

Example: Hamstrings

Lay on your back. With your leg straight, raise it as high as you can. Either scoot through a doorway to have the wall to press against, or have your friend hold your leg in that position. Now press as hard as you can into the wall or your friend's shoulder. Next raise your leg as high as you can (it should be able to go higher now) and scoot further into the doorway with your foot against the wall, or have your partner hold your leg and stretch it 10 seconds. Now push into the wall or your partner's shoulder 10 seconds as hard as you can. Lift your leg even higher (you can do it!) and repeat the process. This or the next round is the last time. Before you lower your leg have your friend (need a friend for this part) push your fully straightened leg back down to the ground while shaking it. Your partner (pushing and shaking your leg) should be able to overpower you. It will take creativity to do this for other areas but you can figure it out – it's worth it!

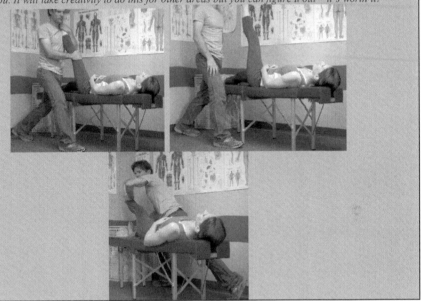

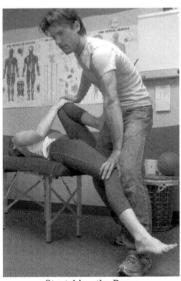

Stretching the Psoas

Below is a list of body areas to stretch. Be sure you know how to do these stretches safely. One stretch per muscle groups is enough, although some body areas require a few stretches due to the multi-joint nature of the area.

WHOLE BODY STRETCHES
Brugger's Relief Pose
A combo of a chin tuck, wall angel, and a pelvic tilt – Brugger's relief posture is a full body exercise. The purpose is to over-do "perfect posture" and hold it as a stretch. This can really help reduce stress and provide some "postural relief". Perform this pose for 15 seconds every few hours throughout the day for full effect. Sit or stand with feet shoulder width apart and slightly turned out (hips externally rotated). Actively press your feet into the ground to increase your foot arch without curling your toes (see "Short Foot" under foot rehab). Find Neutral Pelvis and engage your abs. Rest your arms at your side with elbows straight and palms facing forward. Keep your shoulders down, shoulder blades pulled together and down (like a wall angel) and lift your chest up (like military posture). Finally perform a chin tuck. Remember to breathe! For an extra stretch, put your hands and or knees between a loop of tubing or exercise band.

NECK STRETCHES
Neck Stretch
Keeping your shoulders down, pull your head to the side with your hand. Switch sides. Now pull your head down and slightly towards the arm that is pulling.

Upper Trap and Levator Scapula Stretch
There are several good ways to stretch. One is to grab your wrist behind your back and pull it down while bending your head forward and away from the depressed shoulder. Another way is to grab the side of your chair and lean away from that arm while trying to touch the opposite ear to the opposite shoulder.

WRIST AND FINGER STRETCHES

Flexor Stretch
Shown: on floor, standard stretch, prayer in front and behind, and a palm stretch.

LUMBAR STRETCHES

Cat and Camel
On you hands and knees, arch and flatten your back.

Sphinx or Cobra
On your stomach, press your torso up using your hands.

Active Knee to Chest
Pull both knees into your chest and lightly "pump" your knees further into your chest.

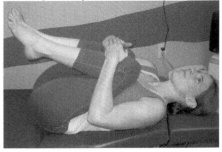

Extension on a Ball
Slowly roll the ball up and down your spine.

Flexion on a Ball
Slowly roll the ball up and down your torso.

Side Flexion on a Ball
Be careful not to fall off!

Lumbar Rotation Supine
Lay on your back either on the floor, or on the edge of a mattress for an extra stretch. Grab your knee opposite your arm (with the other leg straight), and pull it across your body. Try and keep your upper back anchored on the ground. Your back may "pop." Don't bounce or force the stretch to get your back to pop.

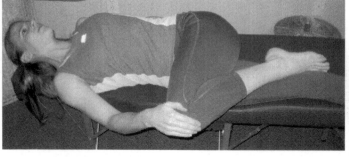

Lumbar Rotation Seated
Sitting on the floor or chair cross your right leg (or visa versa) over your left leg. Take your left hand and place it on your right kneecap. Now turn your torso to the right.

SHOULDER STRETCHES
Rhomboid Stretch
Interlock your fingers with your palms out and really push away from your chest. If that doesn't work, turn your palms towards you, hook your knee, and use your knee to push. Tuck your head down and try to let your upper back "go" by rounding it.

 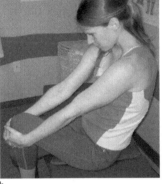

Posterior Capsule Stretch
The easiest way to stretch behind your shoulder joint is to put your arm across your chest and hook it with the inside of your other elbow. Pull your arm in with the other arm. You can also lie on the affected side with your arm around and roll your body towards the outstretched arm.

Behind the Back Towel Stretch
Use a towel if you can't accomplish the stretch without one. Behind your back, grab a towel with both hands and work your hands together for maximum stretch. If possible, your can interlock fingers without a towel.

Whole Arm Doorway or Wall Stretch
Stand in a doorway or next to a wall with your arm outstretched. Place your fingertips against the doorway or wall and walk forward until you feel a stretch from your fingertips to your chest.

79

Pectoralis (Pecs) Corner Stretch
Stand in a doorway with your arm and elbow at 90 degrees. Lay your entire forearm against the side of the door way and step forward until you feel a stretch in your chest.

Subscapularis and Latissimus (Lats) Stretch
Grab your elbow behind your head, and pull it towards your hand.

External Rotator Stretch
Put one elbow inside the other and externally rotate the elbow on top.

Lats Stretch
Shown: child's pose, at your desk or table top.

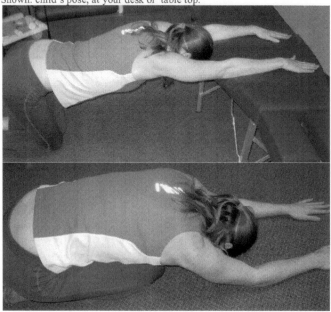

Shoulder Circles
Lightly bring your shoulders up, but not all the way up to your ears. Now pull your shoulder blades together and down. Hold for a second and repeat.

LEG AND HIP STRETCHES
Psoas Stretch
Standing in a fencer's position or kneeling on one knee, gently lunge forward, pivoting on the flexed knee out in front (you are stretching the hip on the leg that is behind). Keep your back straight and chest in military posture. For an added stretch, raise the arm over your head on the side being stretched.

81

Quadriceps (Quads) Stretch

Kneeling or standing grab your ankle and pull it towards your buttocks.

Hamstring Stretch

This is the safest, most effective hamstring stretch. Find a chair or stair that is about knee height. Put your heel up on the chair or stair with your knee locked and leg straight. Your back leg should be completely in line with your torso. Keeping your back totally straight, bend forward at your hips (do not bend your back). To get more hamstring and less calf, point your foot and or unlock your knee slightly. To stretch all of your hamstrings, try turning the involved leg in and out.

Another safe hamstring stretch is to find a doorway, and place your involved leg up against the wall with your body laying inside the doorway. Press your leg firmly into the wall for 10 seconds. Now scoot into the doorway a bit more to increase the stretch. Repeat until you can't get any more length out of your muscle. This is almost identical to the MET stretch described at the beginning of the chapter.

Adductors and Groin Stretch
Shown sitting or supine.

Iliotibial Band (ITB) and Tensor Fascia Latae (TFL) Stretch
Massage your ITB on a foam roller or stretch it standing.

 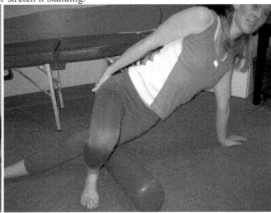

Calf Stretch
The easiest way to stretch you calf is to place the ball of your foot on the edge of a stair and lower your heel down. Another way is to place the ball of your foot up against the wall with your other leg back.

 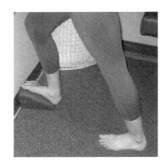 

Piriformis Stretch

The same stretch can be done in several positions: sitting, supine, prone, or standing. I will describe the seated for simplicity. Cross your right leg over your left with your foot as close to being on top of your knee as possible ("figure 4" position). Press firmly down on the bent leg. Keeping your back in a straight "military" position, slowly bend forward at the hips (do not bend your spine).

Gluts

Lay on your back and pull your knee either to the same or opposite shoulder, finding the area of maximum tightness.

 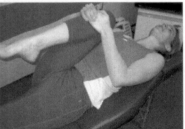

SCHEDULING

The following pages outline when to do each of the climbing, weight, and cardio routines. Ma[...]
following pages, or copy them into a training log. Be sure to warm up, cool down, and stretch aft[...]
Remember, cardio workouts are generally better after climbing or weight training for the hypertrophy[...]
but during maximum recruitment and power-endurance stages it is best to do your cardio before the work[...]

It's a good plan to divide the weights into two groups (A and B) combining core, upper body, and lower body exercises, trying to work all major muscle groups in each group. Repeat exercises in both groups A and B if there isn't an alternate exercise for that muscle group. Fill in any extra time with moderate aerobic and foundation climbing exercises.

Ancient Arts, Fisher Towers Utah. Bill Ahbnum Photo

LIST OF EXERCISES

LOWER BODY:
Squats
One Leg Squats
Step-Ups
Leg Press
Wall Squats
Lunges
Dynamic Lunges
Calf Raises
Hamstring Curls

CORE:
Chin Retraction
Deep Neck Flexion
Reverse Wrist Curls
Finger Extension
Supination and Pronation
Radial and Ulnar Deviation
Reverse Dips
Serratus Punch
Push-Ups Plus
Wide-Grip Lat Pull
Angels
Prone Shoulder Flexion
Sword and Seatbelt
Gorilla Pull
Pelvic Tilt Track
Supine Track
Quadruped Track
Prone Track
Bridge Track
Side Bridge Track
Side-Lying Track
Abdominal Track

HYPERTROPHY:
Pull-Ups
Lat Pulls
Bicep Curls
Bench Press
Rows
Finger Curls
Step-Ups
One Leg Squats
Squats
Leg Press
Hamstring Curls
Calf Raises
Hammer Swing

MAXIMUM RECRUITMENT AND POWER ENDURANCE:
Pull-Ups
Lat Pulls
Bicep Curls
Bench Press
Rows
Finger Curls
Squats
Leg Press

STRETCHES
BODY:
Brugger's Relief
NECK:
Neck Stretch
Upper Trap/Levator Scapula
WRIST AND FINGER:
Wrist/Finger Flexor
BACK:
Cat and Camel
Sphinx or Cobra
Active Knee to Chest
Extension on a Ball
Flexion on a Ball
Side Flexion on a Ball
Lumbar Rotation Supine
Lumbar Rotation Seated
SHOULDER:
Rhomboids
Posterior Capsule
Towel Shoulder Stretch
Doorway or Wall Arm Stretch
Pectoralis Corner Stretch
Subscapularis or Lats
External Rotator
Lats
Shoulder Circles
LEG AND HIP:
Psoas
Quadriceps
Hamstring
Adductors and Groin
ITB and TFL
Calf
Piriformis
Gluts

CARDIO
Moderate Aerobic
Aerobic Threshold
Anaerobic Threshold

TECHNIQUE
Velcro Gloves
No-Hands Climbing
Straight-Arm Climbing
Dynamic Climbing
Open Feet
Add-On

FOUNDATION:
General Climbing
Uninterrupted Climbing

HYPERTROPHY:
Beginning Hangboard
Advanced Hangboard
Ice Tool Hangs

MAXIMUM RECRUITMENT:
Deadpoint
Single Dyno
Double Dyno
Drop Downs
No Feet Bouldering
Speed Climbing
Rope Ladder
Ice Climbing Plyometrics

POWER ENDURANCE:
Repetitive Hold Climbing
Limit or Beyond Climbing
Weighted Climbing
Progressive Bouldering
Repetitive Bouldering

WEIGHT TRAINING
UPPER BODY:
Pull-Ups
Negative Pull-Ups
Staggered Pull-Ups
Lock-Offs
Dynamic Pull-Ups
Lat Pulls
Bicep Curls
Push-Ups
Bench Press
Rows
Triceps Curl
One-Arm Pull-Down
Hammer Swing
Finger Curls
Wrist Curls
Weighted Dowel Roll
Farmer's Cary

FOUNDATION STAGE: WEEK 1-6

Start Date ____/____   End Date ____/____

Foundation Climbing x2	M T W R F Sa Su
General Weights and Core x3	M T W R F Sa Su
Moderate Aerobic x4	M T W R F Sa Su
Foundation Climbing x3	M T W R F Sa Su
General Weights and Core x3	M T W R F Sa Su
Moderate Aerobic x3	M T W R F Sa Su
Foundation Climbing x3	M T W R F Sa Su
General Weights and Core x3	M T W R F Sa Su
Moderate Aerobic x4	M T W R F Sa Su
Foundation Climbing x4	M T W R F Sa Su
General Weights and Core x3	M T W R F Sa Su
Moderate Aerobic x3	M T W R F Sa Su
Foundation Climbing x4	M T W R F Sa Su
General Weights and Core x3	M T W R F Sa Su
Moderate Aerobic x4	M T W R F Sa Su
Foundation Climbing x4	M T W R F Sa Su
General Weights and Core x3	M T W R F Sa Su
Moderate Aerobic x3	M T W R F Sa Su

HYPERTROPHY STAGE: WEEKS 7-11

Start Date ____/____   End Date ____/____

Hypertrophy Climb x2	M T W R F Sa Su
Hypertrophy Weights x2	M T W R F Sa Su
Aerobic Threshold x3	M T W R F Sa Su
Core x2	M T W R F Sa Su
Hypertrophy Climb x2	M T W R F Sa Su
Hypertrophy Weights x2	M T W R F Sa Su
Aerobic Threshold x3	M T W R F Sa Su
Core x2	M T W R F Sa Su
Hypertrophy Climb x2	M T W R F Sa Su
Hypertrophy Weights x2	M T W R F Sa Su
Aerobic Threshold x3	M T W R F Sa Su
Core x2	M T W R F Sa Su
Hypertrophy Climb x2	M T W R F Sa Su
Hypertrophy Weights x2	M T W R F Sa Su
Aerobic Threshold x3	M T W R F Sa Su
Core x2	M T W R F Sa Su
Hypertrophy Climb x2	M T W R F Sa Su
Hypertrophy Weights x2	M T W R F Sa Su
Aerobic Threshold x3	M T W R F Sa Su
Core x2	M T W R F Sa Su

MAXIMUM RECRUITMENT STAGE: WEEKS 12-15

Start Date _____/_____   End Date _____/_____

Max Recruit Climb x2	M T W R F Sa Su
Max Recruit Weights x2	M T W R F Sa Su
Anaerobic Threshold x1-2	M T W R F Sa Su
Core x2	M T W R F Sa Su
Max Recruit Climb x2	M T W R F Sa Su
Max Recruit Weights x2	M T W R F Sa Su
Anaerobic Threshold x1-2	M T W R F Sa Su
Core x2	M T W R F Sa Su
Max Recruit Climb x2	M T W R F Sa Su
Max Recruit Weights x2	M T W R F Sa Su
Anaerobic Threshold x1-2	M T W R F Sa Su
Core x2	M T W R F Sa Su
Max Recruit Climb x2	M T W R F Sa Su
Max Recruit Weights x2	M T W R F Sa Su
Anaerobic Threshold x1-2	M T W R F Sa Su
Core x2	M T W R F Sa Su

POWER ENDURANCE STAGE: WEEKS 16-19

Start Date _____/_____   End Date _____/_____

Climb Power Endurance x2	M T W R F Sa Su
Power Endurance Weights x2	M T W R F Sa Su
Aerobic Threshold x1	M T W R F Sa Su
Anaerobic Threshold x1	M T W R F Sa Su
Core x1	M T W R F Sa Su
Climb Power Endurance x2	M T W R F Sa Su
Power Endurance Weights x2	M T W R F Sa Su
Aerobic Threshold x1	M T W R F Sa Su
Anaerobic Threshold x1	M T W R F Sa Su
Core x1	M T W R F Sa Su
Climb Power Endurance x2	M T W R F Sa Su
Power Endurance Weights x2	M T W R F Sa Su
Aerobic Threshold x1	M T W R F Sa Su
Anaerobic Threshold x1	M T W R F Sa Su
Core x1	M T W R F Sa Su
Climb Power Endurance x2	M T W R F Sa Su
Power Endurance Weights x2	M T W R F Sa Su
Aerobic Threshold x1	M T W R F Sa Su
Anaerobic Threshold x1	M T W R F Sa Su
Core x1	M T W R F Sa Su

RECOVERY: WEEKS 20-22

Start Date ____/____   End Date ____/____

Foundation Climbing x2	M T W R F Sa Su
General Weights x2	M T W R F Sa Su
Moderate Aerobic x3	M T W R F Sa Su
Foundation Climbing x1	M T W R F Sa Su
General Weights x1	M T W R F Sa Su
Moderate Aerobic x2	M T W R F Sa Su
Rest and Carb Load	M T W R F Sa Sun

2ND CYCLE = 10 WEEKS
3 weeks Foundation, 2 weeks Hypertrophy, 2 weeks Maximum Recruitment, 2 weeks Power-Endurance, 1 week Rest

3RD CYCLE = 6 WEEKS
2 weeks Hypertrophy, 2 weeks Maximum Recruitment, 1 week Power Endurance, 1 week Rest

Ruth Gorge, Alaska
Cory Bennett Photo

CHAPTER TWO:
INJURIES

Castle Crags, CA

If you climb on a regular basis, you will inevitably get injured. Younger climbers, those with impeccable technique, and the very lucky are the exceptions. When you get injured, you will be glad you had a fantastic baseline of fitness to speed up your recovery. This section cannot replace personalized advice and care from a qualified medical practitioner. However, I have included several effective types of conservative treatment for common climbing injuries. It does not hurt to suggest these treatments I have described to your health care provider. If your doctor or health care provider is not helping you get better, it is well within your rights as a patient to get a second, third or fourth opinion.

I took a different approach on this chapter. Instead of writing about individual injuries and their specific treatments, I focused more on the treatments themselves since they have so much cross-over between injuries. If you have an injury then read about what kind of injury you have, the treatment options, and finally who you may want to see.

WHO SHOULD YOU SEE?

The worst thing you can do is nothing, so I will discuss some different medical specialists and why you might choose them. I'm pretty sure I'll ruffle some feathers here since I do have my own opinions on these professions and what they are best for. They all have their place, and our health care system would suffer without any of them. Some specialists think they are the best at pretty much every aspect of health care and think that you'd be a fool to see someone else. It's the old hammer metaphor (if all you have is a hammer everything starts looking like nails). Bottom line: shop around. Start with the least invasive and most inexpensive treatment options available. If you think it's serious, then see a doctor who best fits the area of complaint that you can see quickly. If it's life threatening, go to the emergency room or call 911.

Chiropractic Doctors (DC)
Ok, so I'm a little biased since I am one. Chiropractors are primary care physicians with extensive medical training and can diagnose and treat a surprising amount of conditions. Their primary focus is to get you better without resorting to surgery or prescription medications. A good chiropractor knows his or her scope, and will refer to surgeons, specialists, and MD's for prescriptions if necessary. Chiropractors' main therapy is to use joint manipulation in order to restore motion, function, and proper biomechanics to the spine and extremities. They also use all of the same methods that physical therapists utilize in most states. Chiropractors also dispense nutritional and lifestyle advice from a medical perspective. In some states chiropractors perform routine blood and urine tests, deliver babies, and perform minor surgical procedures. The stigma around chiropractic originates from the late 1800's when the profession was formed. Chiropractors then claimed joint dysfunction as the source of all physical ailments (MDs still used leaches and cranial measurement at this time remember). There are a few today who still cling to this dated theory, and are unfortunately some of the outspoken ones that taint the profession.

Naturopathic Doctors (ND)
Like Chiropractors, Naturopaths are doctors with extensive medical training and similar scopes of practice. Instead of joint manipulation and physical therapy, their treatment of choice is to prescribe natural medications, deliver injections (prolotherapy for instance), and to treat with nutritional intake modifications.

Medical Doctors (MD)
With an almost unlimited scope of practice, medical doctors come in all shapes, sizes, and specialties. Their primary treatment method is prescription medication and surgical procedures. They are especially useful in life or death situations and diagnosing complex medical problems according to their specialty. Family practice MD's are great for routine physicals, antibiotics, minor health problems, and routing you to a specialist. For more complex health problems, it's best to go directly to a specialist (assuming you know what type of specialist you need). Depending on the injury, climbers will most likely see orthopedic surgeons for surgery on musculoskeletal injuries, neurologists for injuries with complex neurological problems, or emergency doctors for life threatening injuries and first-aid. There are many other specialists like rheumatologists for auto-immune disease, oncologists for cancer, dermatologists for skin conditions, physiatrists for chronic pain, cardiologists for heart and vascular conditions, any many more. If you are in serious medical need, need surgery, or have a disease, then MD's are your best bet.

Osteopathic Doctors (DO)
Most osteopaths perform the same function (that is they are identical to) as medical doctors, but some (but not many) also perform spinal adjustments similar to chiropractors.

Physical Therapists (PT)

Physical therapists are a lot like chiropractors, except they best specialize in rehabbing post-surgical patients. There are some DPT's (doctor of physical therapy). DPT's are like a PhD in physical therapy, but in most states, they do not have the same scope of practice (like diagnosis) as the above professions. If you need longer one-on-one sessions for rehab, then a PT's are your best bet.

Massage Therapists (LMT)

There are many different styles of massage therapy, some are very specialized and have little ^{TM} symbols above their specialty. If your problem is chronically tight muscles and could use an hour of therapy, see a massage therapist. There are some amazing massage therapists out there and can provide more benefit than any doctor ever could.

Personal Trainers

Personal trainers generally work in gyms or health clubs. They are excellent recourses to get you motivated to work out. Although there are some fantastic trainers out there in the bigger franchise gyms, be wary. It's ok to ask for their experience and credentials. If you lack motivation and want to get whipped into shape, or you are a gym newbie, get yourself a personal trainer.

Acupuncturists (LAc)

A truly eastern practice that defies the term "medical", acupuncturists use needles to stimulate your nervous system (or chi). They are fantastic for chronic pain or general stress, or when nothing else has worked in the past.

Nurses and Physicians' Assistants (RN, LNP, or PA)

Nurses and PA's are quickly becoming the portal of entry health practitioner in medical clinics and hospitals. Most can even prescribe medication under the license of an MD or DO. Nurse Practitioners can prescribe without the supervision of a Medical Doctor. These are some of healthcare's hardest working professionals.

Diagnosis: History, Physical, Imaging, Testing

The first thing your doctor should do is to ask you a lot of questions. Be "patient" and don't unload your entire history on him or her until the end if anything was missed you feel important. Next the physician needs to actually look at the area of complaint. The area should be palpated, and then put through a battery of orthopedic tests. Orthopedic tests stress an area to rule in or out a possible diagnosis. Sometimes it is not all that obvious, the treatment just isn't working, or not enough information is gathered in the history and exam. This is when you want an image of the area. X-rays are as cheap as dirt, show you hard tissues like bone, but do not show soft tissues like muscles, tendons, fluid, and cartilage. MRI's are much more expensive, but show the underlying soft tissues. CT's are basically 3-D x-rays and can show some structure that x-rays and MRI's cannot. If your doctor skipped important questions, didn't look at or palpate the area, breezed over the orthopedic tests, or didn't do any imagining it is well within your right to say something like, "why didn't you take an x-ray?" or "I would like an MRI". Avoid the know-it-all doctor who can magically diagnosis your injury without going through the steps. Your injury may seem textbook to the doctor, but they may be missing what's really going on. Illness and disease are almost the sole reason you would get laboratory testing. Even though disease can mimic musculoskeletal injury, discussing this further is way beyond the scope of this book. Your doctor should also offer all possible treatment options.

Ouray, CO. Jay Hack Photo

TREATMENT

If you are seriously injured go to the emergency room or call 911 immediately! If life or limb is not immediately threatened and you feel the need to see someone, make the appointment sooner than later. Sometimes the cure is worse than the disease, so do your homework and research who to see and what can be done. No book can take the place of expert advice from a qualified health care professional. In the end it is your body that heals you, all health care professionals can do is help your body with this process. The following treatments listed can be applied to just about every injury discussed below, so try them out.

P.R.I.C.E IS RIGHT

This handy acronym lays out the initial steps to take when injured.

Protect

This can mean splints, braces, wraps, bandages, or even casts. The most important factor of "Protect" is to change or avoid the aggravating activity. Most climbing injuries occur from overuse, poor form, or a combination of both. This can be extremely subtle. For instance, if you blow out your shoulder, maybe you need to stop dynoing, calm down on the off-widths, improve your footwork, stretch, or strengthen your shoulder stabilizers.

Rest

This goes along with Protect. Stop doing what caused the injury! Your body needs time to heal (3-4 days at the minimum for a new injury to get out of the acute inflammation phase). If you hurt your fingers, maybe now is a good time to improve your cardio and dust off those trail running shoes. I always emphasize an "active rest" after the initial acute stage of healing has passed (minimum 3-4 days). Movement is life, so get things moving as soon as you can – but STOP when it hurts.

Ice

Twenty minutes on followed by one hour off is the golden rule for icing an area. Inflammation basically means "on fire". So do things to put out that fire! Ice cubes in a baggie are the easiest, chemical ice packs are nice but you may need to put a towel between it and your skin since they get much colder than ice. Bags of frozen vegetables work great and retain the cold quite a long time. I think frozen corn kernels are the best choice.

Ice Massage is a great way to combine ice therapy with cross friction massage (see below). The easiest way to do this is freeze some water in a Dixie cup, peel back the edges so the ice is exposed and the cup acts as the handle. Rub the affected area back and forth with the ice for up to 20 minutes. It will at first feel cold, then painful, then burning, and finally numb.

Heat can help for chronic injuries or tight muscles, but can do more harm than good if the injury is acute. Heat promotes blood flow which is helpful in chronic conditions but harmful in the acute stages. If in doubt ice. Except in cases of hypothermia, neurological damage, or severe burns you can't go wrong with ice.

Compress

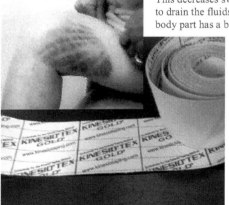

This decreases swelling. You don't want to cut off circulation, but you want to drain the fluids in your tissue that are products of inflammation. Each body part has a best type of compress – but in general, an ace-wrap works well everywhere. A product called "Kinesio Tape" is one of the latest and greatest inventions to reduce swelling, limit motion, and provide proprioceptive feedback. The sticky, stretchy, waterproof tape is specially designed to create a negative pressure between your skin and fascia, thus improving lymphatic and venous flow to decrease swelling and bruising. Its stretchy properties check your active range of motion, limiting your movement like athletic tape, but allowing full use of the joint.

Shown: Bruise Reduced with Kinesiotape

Elevate
For more serious injuries, elevating your affected limb helps to decrease swelling and pooling of blood and fluid.

ELECTRICAL MODALITIES
These therapies, often performed by Chiropractors and Physical Therapists have been proven to decrease inflammation and promote tissue repair.

Ultrasound
Ultrasound is the old standby, and it acts as both a deep heating modality and as a mechanical force (via sound waves) to decrease swelling, promote healing, and reduce scar tissue.

Cold Laser and L.E.D. Light Therapy
These are the new kids on the block, but the research is showing better results than ultrasound. Cold laser is also a deep heating modality, but instead of using sound waves,

cold laser uses light to stimulate your cells to promote healing. I know it sounds "mystical" but this is one of those things that actually works, and works well. There are many different types of cold laser, from pen lights to large machines. L.E.D. lights are often used in conjunction with cold laser, and have been shown to be extremely effective as well. Try and find a practitioner that has both L.E.D. and Cold Laser. Cold laser and L.E.D. work great on cuts and on deeper injuries that are hard to do anything else on (except surgery) like the inside of your knees or shoulders.

Microcurrent
This electrical modality has fallen out of fashion, mostly due to the advent of cold laser. However, tiny microcurrent units can be purchased and worn all day, unlike the other electrical modalities discussed. Healing time can be sped up considerably with Microcurrent, and it is still a great tool to get better quicker. Microcurrent acts on similar principles as Cold Laser as it helps speed up healing times in injured areas.

Electrical Muscle Stimulation
There are many different types of Electrical Muscle Stimulation, and it's up to your Chiro or PT to decide what type to use. E-Stim can be used as a nerve block, as a pump to decrease swelling, as a rehab tool to retrain and rehab muscles, and as a way to relax hypertonic muscles and reduce trigger points. E-stim machines help relax muscles and trigger points so the health care provider can follow up with other treatments that require them to 'dig in deeper'. Different forms of electrical stimulation include Galvanic, High-Volt, Biphasic, Sine, and IFC (Interferential). One form of E-stim, Galvanic, can be used to push ions into your skin, muscle, and

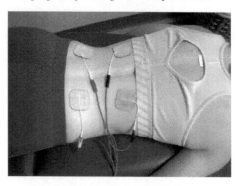

blood. This is usually used to deliver pain and anti-inflammatory medication. This is called Iontophoresis. Ultrasound can be used to similar ends, and this is called Phonophoresis. I'm always asked about using E-Stim to train (like Bruce Lee popularized). Russian Stimulation Current can be used to strength train, but is extremely time consuming and can be expensive to obtain a unit. If you complete every phase of this training manual and are as strong as you'll ever get via climbing and weight lifting, then consider this option. Unfortunately, it can't be used as a shortcut to training – sorry.

T.E.N.S. (Transcutaneus Neural Stimulation)
These portable units are a type of E-stim that can also be worn, but they really only work well as a nerve block to help with pain.

94

Other Electrical Modalities

There are many other electrical physical therapy devices out there that are effective such as fluidotherapy, whirlpool baths, paraffin wax, infrared, U.V., and diathermy, but I feel they are more suited for acute post-surgical rehab, for special needs, or geriatric patients.

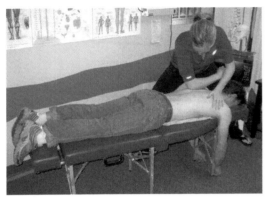

MASSAGE

Everybody needs a massage! But besides as a pampering device, and relaxation for tight muscles, massage can promote healing for injured muscles. Below are some effective techniques. Buyer Beware! There a hundreds of techniques, many of them are even trademarked. Many techniques have "cookbook" formulas and prescribe an exact number of sessions. Most techniques are variations on a theme. The techniques listed below have a myriad amount of variations and each practitioner will have his or her own spin.

Deep Tissue Massage (Includes: Rolfing, Muscle Energy, and Active Release Techniques)

The basic tenants of deep tissue massage is to break up scar tissue, release adhesions, reduce trigger points, promote blood flow, decrease edema, and eliminate toxins (no matter what your yoga teacher may tell you, sweating is a very ineffective way to eliminate toxins). This can hurt, but it should be a "good hurt". Don't begin this therapy until after the acute state is over, and inflammation has been addressed.

Rolfing

Rolfing is a great deep tissue technique, and is one of the few trademarked techniques that have proven very effective. Most Rolfer's don't just focus on one area; rather they have a 10-session formula covering your entire body (including a sinus treatment). If you are trying to rehab a specific area, tell your massage therapist to focus there and address the rest of your body at a later date.

Muscle Energy Techniques

These active stretching techniques are basically advanced stretching with aid of a practitioner (see the stretching section). The goal is that by actively contacting agonist and antagonist muscle groups, you can trick your nervous system's complex array of stretch and reflex receptors (golgi tendon organs, muscle spindles, and reflex arcs) to relax a muscle that is hypertonic. Most muscles are tight but not short. That is, the muscle is constantly in a state of over-contraction. You first need to have the muscle relax before you can physically lengthen it.

Active Release Technique (A.R.T., Pin and Stretch)

A.R.T. is a trademarked technique, also known as "Pin and Stretch" (not-trademarked). It is a type of deep tissue massage with active involvement of the patient. Basically the practitioner squeezes a contracted muscle while the patient tries to lengthen it. This is a gross oversimplification, but the basic motive is to relax tight muscles, reduce trigger points, and break up scar tissue.

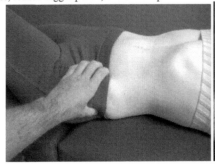 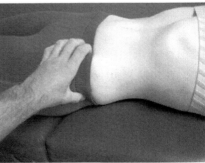

Cross-Friction, Graston, Gua Sha

When your body rebuilds damaged tissue, it lays down fibers in a haphazard fashion initially (like a duct-tape patch job), and this is what scar tissue is. After a month or so, your body remodels the scar tissue. However, this job doesn't always get accomplished properly and complete remodeling can take a year or much longer. These techniques greatly speed up the remodeling process, help to reduce scar tissue initially, and can help with chronic pain. These therapies are extremely effective and should be utilized as soon as the acute stage is over (2-4 days to 12 weeks depending on the injury). Cross friction technique involves rubbing an involved area (usually a tendon) perpendicular to the fibers for up to 20 minutes.

Cross friction seems to work best on injuries with larger exposed tendons and ligaments (like the one just below your kneecap). Graston and Gua Sha, are essentially synonymous, but Graston uses expensive instruments and has been trademarked. Graston is one of the "latest and greatest" tools for tissue repair. Unlike cross-friction, a Graston practitioner generally follows the direction of the fiber (muscle, tendon, or ligament) to remove scar tissue, adhesions, and promote healing. Gua Sha follows the same theory, but uses different instruments and is generally less aggressive. I highly recommend a trial of several treatments with either technique for muscle, ligament, and tendon injuries.

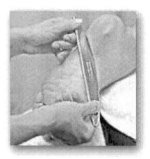  

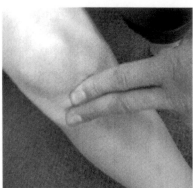 

Top: Graston Technique. Bottom: Cross Friction and Gua Sha

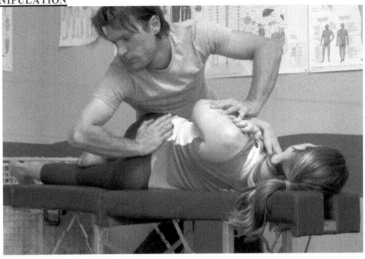

Although some states allow physical therapists to perform this therapy, and MD's and Osteopaths can as well, I strongly urge you to see a sports chiropractor. Reported cases of injury are surprisingly low (chiropractors' malpractice insurance are just about the cheapest in the medical profession), but a chiropractor's training on this technique is unsurpassed.

There are several benefits to joint mobilization (aka an "Adjustment"). The first is pain relief. If a joint is subluxated (that is partially dislocated) it's going to hurt. This is especially true in the spine. Also, if a joint is "stuck", the mechanoreceptors (cells in joints that signal proprioceptive input to your brain) will start signaling pain instead. Muscles will brace and guard the area, causing increased pain and tightness.

Joints that are stuck or in the wrong position can also cause improper biomechanics, and this can lead to dysfunction. Think about your tires. If they aren't properly aligned, you could blow a tire. Your car will also not be as efficient. The same principals relate to your structure. Your spine provides the basic framework for your entire body, and small misalignments can cause big problems in many areas. The same is true for the other joints in your body – especially your feet.

97

Joint manipulation has an effect on your nervous system. Pain, numbness, or tingling in your arms, legs, head, etc, comes from nerve irritation (very rarely is it because of decreased blood flow). This irritation can come from your spinal cord, or from the nerves that exit your spinal cord between your vertebrae. Even slight pressure on these nerves can cause pain, numbness, tingling, or weakness – and major pressure like that of a disc herniation can cause serious complications. Poor posture and or spinal misalignments cause this pressure.

Occasionally organs can be affected. The same nerves that exit your spine that cause pain or tingling also are the nerves that control all the other functions in your body. For instance, people with disc herniations commonly suffer from incontinence because the nerves that control bowel and bladder function are being compressed.

Finally, joints that move properly and have correct biomechanics should not develop arthritis or fuse. Climber's backs and necks have a lot of postural problems, and long term consequences can be degenerative joint disease and spinal fusion due to an increased amount of pressure. The body lays down material to protect an area that has an un-physiologic amount of pressure (like callus on your hands, or bunions on you feet). In your spine, your body adds more bone (spurs) until it fused the area to protect it. Loss of normal spinal curves can cause these changes over time. The bottom line: Problems with the biomechanics in your body can cause pain, numbness, tingling, weakness, arthritis, neurological, and visceral problems.

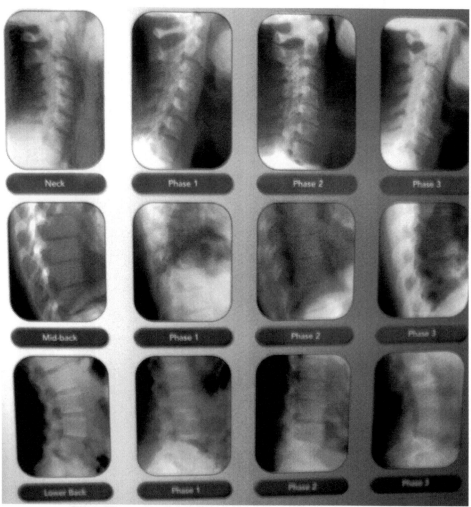

Chart of Progressive Spinal Degeneration Due to Biomechanical Stresses

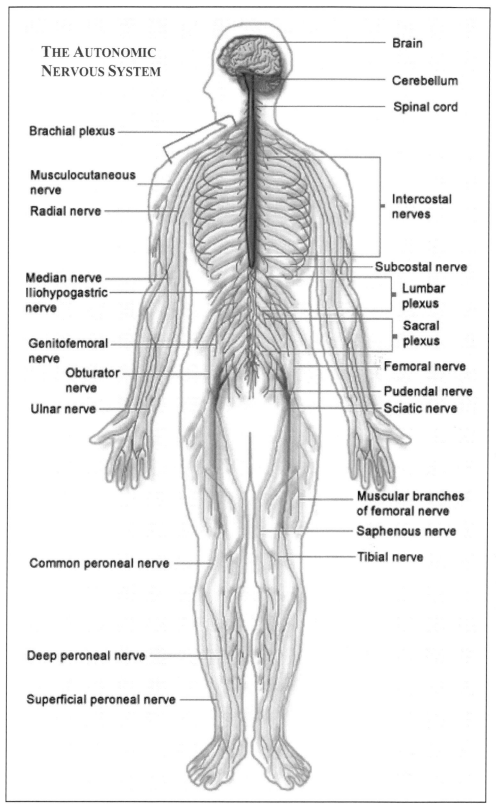

THE AUTONOMIC
NERVOUS SYSTEM

Brain

Cerebellum

Spinal cord

Brachial plexus

Musculocutaneous nerve

Radial nerve

Intercostal nerves

Median nerve

Iliohypogastric nerve

Subcostal nerve

Lumbar plexus

Sacral plexus

Genitofemoral nerve

Obturator nerve

Ulnar nerve

Femoral nerve

Pudendal nerve

Sciatic nerve

Muscular branches of femoral nerve

Saphenous nerve

Tibial nerve

Common peroneal nerve

Deep peroneal nerve

Superficial peroneal nerve

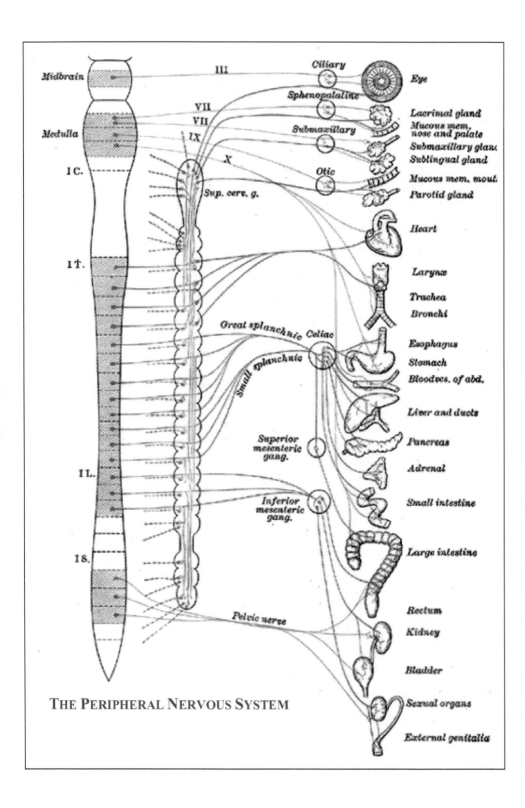

THE PERIPHERAL NERVOUS SYSTEM

100

TRACTION

Traction is like stretching for your joints. Traction helps to reduce pressure in a joint, and gradually stretches the muscles, ligaments, and tissues in the area. There are many different formulas for traction, with factors including: duration, load (weight), and loading - unloading cycles.

Traction as a therapy is a great tool for spine and disc problems, headaches, hip pain, shoulder pain, and carpal tunnel syndrome. Traction can sometimes be the key to fixing

Wrist Traction Device

a problem, but it can also make an area much worse! Usually a light trial treatment is performed to see how an area will react. Two people with identical problems could have completely different results.

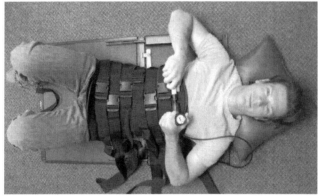

Low back Traction and Neck Traction

PAIN KILLERS AND ANTI-INFLAMMATORY MEDICATION
Note: Before taking any prescribed or over-the-counter drug or supplement consult with your heath care practitioner to rule out any contraindications or adverse reactions you may experience. Even the most harmless drug can cause an adverse reaction or allergic reaction. Remember, almost all drugs treat symptoms and do not cure. Use caution! See the Nutrition section for more information.

NSAIDS
These drugs, when taken at appropriate doses, help decrease inflammation, and can help with pain. They can also poison your liver and damage your bowels. They can also kill you. There is evidence that they also hinder post-acute state repair, especially muscle fibers. So taking them after a hard work-out can be counter-productive. Another factor is the dose. Depending on the NSAID, taking a couple pills may not actually do anything for inflammation. Check with your doctor or pharmacist for specific doses to achieve an anti-inflammatory effect. Common NSAIDS are: Aspirin, Ibuprofen, and Naproxen (Aleve). NSAIDS are a great "quick fix", although they really don't fix anything.

Opiates and Muscle Relaxers
Although these can make you feel good, relieve pain, and enhance your Pink Floyd listening experience – prescribed pain killers and muscle relaxers should only be used in cases of extreme pain. They do not cure anything and only help to reduce unbearable pain from serious injuries or surgery. However, it's a good idea to stash a few of these in your med kit for the backcountry, so see if your MD will prescribe you some.

Natural NSAIDS
A bit more pricey, and a little less research, but a whole lot less dangerous for your system – consider finding a blend of natural anti-inflammatory supplements. Some of the best are: Bromelain, Turmeric, White Willow Bark (aspirin comes from this, but the unprocessed form contains natural buffers to limit the adverse effects), Ginger, Boswellia, Devil's Claw, Capsaicin, Green Tea, Grape Seed Extract, Quercetin, and Proteolytic

Enzymes. Cox-2 Support by Victory Nutrition is my favorite blend. PSI Nighttime and Daytime, and Wobenzym are also good proprietary blends.

TISSUE REPAIR SUPPLEMENTS

Antioxidants help greatly with musculoskeletal tissue repair and taking a daily does will help with recovery and general health. A major function of Vitamin C is to build new connective tissue (like your ligaments and tendons), so now is the time to up your dose! Calcium, Magnesium, Zinc, Vitamin D and E, and a B-Vitamin Complex are excellent vitamins to take to promote healing.

For joint problems, try Glucosamine Sulfate or Chondroitin Sulfate. Be sure to get the supplement ending in "Sulfate," not "HCL". Supplements ending in HCL may or may not work - all the clinical trails have been done with the sulfate versions. The jury is still out on the addition of MSM, SamE, or Hyaluronic Acid as helpers for joint and cartilage repair. If buying a supplement with these ingredients, be sure it includes a full dose of Glucosamine (1500mg) or Chondroitin (1200mg). It doesn't matter if you choose Glucosamine or Chondroitin – they both have equal results according to the literature. A nice thing about these supplements is that they have an additive effect. You can take the full dose in the morning (or whenever), instead of spreading it out throughout the day. You can also take a month off without losing the effect, which is nice since these are not cheap. My favorite brand is "Arthriflex Advantage".

There are many other excellent supplements to address health conditions, but it is beyond the scope of this book. Great sources of information can be found at The Linus Pauling Institute: http://lpi.oregonstate.edu/ and Health Notes (accessed for free via GNC's website) http://library.gnc.com/healthnotes/Welcome.aspx?lang=en

TAPING AND BRACING

This falls under the protect, rest, and compress category of PRICE. Injuries like fractures or complete muscle tears will require around 8-12 weeks of complete immobilization to prevent further injury while your body heals. Mild to moderate sprains and strains require much less time in a brace. An injury where the joint is loosened can require two weeks of brace time, even if the area doesn't hurt. Milder sprains and strains either require wearing a brace for a week or two off and on, and chronic or low grade injury may just require bracing during the aggravating activity.

Fingers

Tape your fingers after an injury, or during high load finger specific climbing. Finger braces are generally only used to completely immobilize a finger after a break or moderate to severe sprain.

Wrists

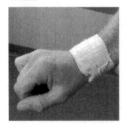

There are quite a few varieties of wrist braces and supports. The wrist brace with aluminum stays that extend up into your forearm are great for acute sprains. For milder wrist sprains, carpal tunnel syndrome, or thumb injuries, use an elastic fingerless glove-like support with an elastic wrist strap and a thumb spica (Futuro makes the best). For chronic wrist sprains or wrist instability, you can use an elastic wrist wrap, or tape your wrist during the aggravating activity.

Elbows

The most common reason to brace an elbow is for a condition called lateral epicondylitis, or golfer's elbow. This nasty condition creates pain in your lateral elbow (the lateral side is with palms facing forward) and can quickly degenerate into a Tendinosis (tendon degeneration and necrosis). An elastic elbow strap with a soft pad built in helps take tension off the muscles attaching to your lateral elbow. Joint manipulation can be very effective for this condition. You can also tape your elbow, but I find this to be too limiting and painful to remove.

Shoulders
The most common shoulder brace is an arm sling. When you require an arm sling, it is very important to use it constantly, usually for a couple weeks. Kinesio Tape is also extremely effective for shoulder injuries.

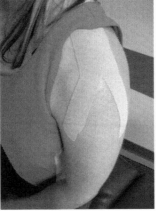 

SI Joint/Low Back
There are literally thousands of devices, chairs, pillows, etc... for low back and Sacroiliac joint problems. I don't recommend using a back brace constantly, even with severe low back or SI joint pain because it de-trains your important stabilizer muscles. People with loose SI joints can benefit from an SI belt worn constantly, however. Wear a back brace only during high risk activities, and try to wean yourself off it as soon as possible. A strong core is as effective as any back brace. Kinesio Taping the low back or SI joint is a great compromise, and can relieve pain substantially.

For low back support, find the least invasive, lowest profile back pillow you can find that relieves the pressure on your spine. If you spend a good deal of time driving, it would be a good idea to have one in your car seat at all times. At work, sitting on an exercise ball can help alleviate back strain and engage your core. It is not a good idea to sit on one 8 hours a day because your back will become over-fatigued, so have a chair available too. Vestibular discs are excellent replacements for exercise balls since they are low profile, can be removed when not in use, and make a great balance board for your feet.

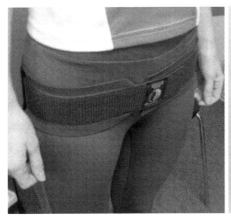 

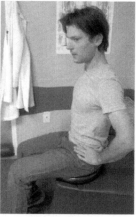

Head and Neck

As a chiropractor, I have never prescribed a neck brace or cervical collar (as seen in television shows where the plaintiff has whiplash). Unless your neck is broken, recovering from surgery, or is completely unstable, don't wear a neck brace. What I recommend is a comfortable pillow that allows your neck to be in a neutral position while sleeping. Firm orthotic versions are available for passive neck stretching, but don't fall asleep on these! Curved pillows may be great for one person, and may cause a stiff neck in the morning for someone else. You can also use a "Jackson Roll", hang your head off the end of the bed while lying on your back (stop if you get dizzy), or roll up a towel to lie on. Lay on your back with the firm or soft neck pillow or orthotic behind your neck. Start slow, and work up to 20 minutes a night. Don't fall asleep on these!

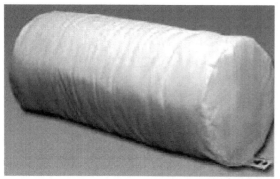

Cervical Roll and Orthotic

Knees

There are as many different types of knee braces as there are for the wrist and low back. For patellar pain, a Chopat-style strap works great. This is basically a piece of surgical tubing inside an elastic band, although the one shown here is fancier. It goes under the knee cap and takes the tension and pressure off of your patella. Taping your patella in a medial direction can also help for patellar tracking problems. For knee instability of post surgery, there are neoprene knee supports with lateral aluminum stays.

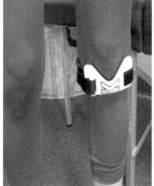

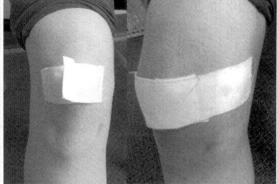

Chopat-Style Knee Brace

Taping the Knee: Make a flap. Use another piece of tape to pull the flap towards the middle.

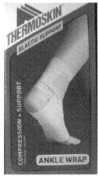

Ankles
For acute injuries, athletic tape works the best. There are several ways to tape, and an inversion strain is the most commonly taped injury. For chronic ankle sprains, there are many different styles of braces. Find what works best for you.

Feet
Some people swear by taping their arches. I feel that this may help in the short term, but in the long run you are weakening your feet. For Plantar Fasciitis, inflammation (although usually a tendinosis) of the bottom of your feet, one of the best treatments is to wear a night splint that stretches your foot and calf. There are socks and low profile braces that have elastic sewn into the toes that pull up on your foot and wrap around your calf. Although the full-on night splint is generally more effective, wearing the sock may be the only thing that allows you to get a good night's sleep!

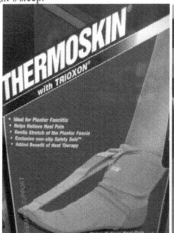
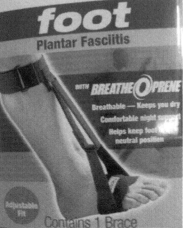

Orthotics
Orthotics are a type of brace for your feet. Orthotics have never fixed anyone's feet, but they can sometimes offer the most reasonable solution (like eyeglasses help your eyes but don't fix the actual problem). Orthotics can help with many physical problems – from foot pain, to shin splints, to low back pain. They are a crutch, and a good pair is not cheap! Start with a pair of non-custom store bought kind first. Studies have show that 80% of problems helped with custom made orthotics have been equally helped with a cheaper store bought kind (like the Superfeet brand). Avoid the middle ground, however! If the cheapies don't work, get a real pair made in a lab. The middle of the road models are usually just very expensive store bought kinds. If it looks gimmicky, it

probably is. There are many other types of foot inserts such as heel lifts, toe spacers, toe caps, heel cups, and metatarsal pads to help with conditions such as heel pain, bunions, hammertoe, metatarsalgia, compacted toe nails, and Hallux Valgus to name a few. A note of caution: make sure your hips or low back aren't the cause for a leg length inequality before using a heel lift.

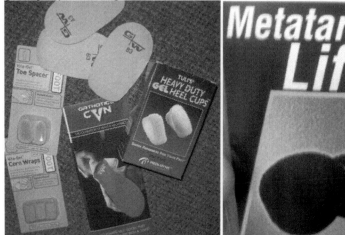

PROLOTHERAPY

This is the treatment of choice for loose joints, tendons, and ligaments when conservative care has failed and surgery isn't yet an option. Naturopathic, Medical, and Osteopathic doctors can perform this treatment. A solution of saline, dextrose (sugar), drugs, and or natural supplements is injected into the joint space or where the tendon or ligament attaches to the bone. This triggers a controlled inflammatory response which stimulates the proliferation of fibroblasts which create new tissue, and increased blood supply to the area. This tightens up the joint capsule, ligament, or tendon. The average number of treatments is around five. It is imperative to find a highly qualified practitioner since there is a fine line because too much scar tissue can build up. After the therapy, the area may require rehab from a chiropractor, PT, or massage therapist to loosen the area back to a physiologic level.

EXERCISE
SEE THE END OF THIS CHAPTER FOR A LIST OF SPECIFIC EXERCISES

Above: Ice applied the wrong way. Ouray, CO.   *Cory Bennett Photo*

TYPES OF INJURY

Treatment varies from injury to injury, but most musculoskeletal injuries can be treated with a mix of the above described treatments. FOR ALMOST ALL INJURIES, USE THE "PRICE" ROUTINE.

CUTS FLAPPERS AND GOBIES
Athletic tape is the treatment of choice in the field. If you can't tape the area, or if you get a flapper, then stash a small vial of a liquid bandage like Liquid Band-Aid or Crazy Glue in your pack for temporarily sealing it shut. Be sure and wash it out with clean soap and water first to avoid trapping in dirt.

TENDONITIS AND TENDINOSIS
Tendonitis is an inflammatory overuse injury of your tendons or ligaments. If left untreated and the overuse continues, the injury can progress (or regress that is) to tendinosis. Tendinosis is when the injury slips into the chronic stage and recovery becomes increasingly difficult. Initial treatment of tendonitis is the PRICE regime. Cortisone injections used to be the treatment of choice for tendonitis, but recently doctors have been cutting back. The problem with cortisone is that it acts like Liquid Plumber for your connective tissue, and is usually only effective for a short time. That said, sometimes a cortisone injection will nip it in the bud. Some doctors will go straight for the cortisone injection, especially if what they are treating is not their specialty – beware of this. Anti-inflammatory medication or supplements, massage, manipulation, cold laser, traction, ultrasound, microcurrent, bracing, and stretching are usually better initial treatments.

BURSITIS
One type of crushing injury caused by climbing is Bursitis. Bursae are fluid filled sacs that protect the outside of joints. They have no direct blood supply or way to drain, so if inflamed, theses painful lumps on your knuckles (from ice climbing), knees, and elbows can take a very long time to heal. Kinesio tape, cold laser, ultrasound, and ice are the treatments of choice.

SPRAINS AND STRAINS
A strain is a torn muscle and a sprain is a torn ligament. A grade I sprain/strain is generally a painful (can be extremely painful making the injury seem a lot worse than it is) minor tear or micro tear that can take a few days to a couple months to fully heal. A grade II is a decent size rip in the fibers and can still heal on its own, although surgery is sometimes necessary. A grade III is a complete tear or rupture and requires surgery. A grade III sprain/strain doesn't always hurt! Recovery from these takes about 12 weeks to a few years to fully heal depending on your age and the type of injury. Treatments listed in the tendonitis section are equally as effective for sprains or strains although bracing is used a bit more here.

BROKEN BONES AND STRESS FRACTURES
There are several different ways a bone can break, but they all heal the same if set properly. Sometimes breaking a bone is a much better fate than grade II or III sprain/strain as soft tissues take much longer to heal. Fractures can heal in as little as 4 weeks, and generally not much longer than 12 (8 being the average). Ways to speed up healing before the cast even comes off are: supplementing with extra calcium, along with the other vitamins and supplements mentioned above, and cold laser and microcurrent.

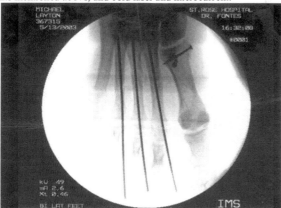

X-Ray of my Right Foot!

NEUROLOGIC MUSCULOSKELETAL PROBLEMS

Musculoskeletal neurological problems are generally due to a compressed, stretched, or irritated nerves. The symptoms are: pain, numbness, tingling, weakness, and or a loss or change in sensations such as light touch, pain, vibration, and temperature. The PRICE rules apply as in any musculoskeletal injury. Vitamin B6 is helpful in some nerve injuries, although too much can actually create the symptoms it treats. Dose is dependent on several factors, so do your research before popping too many B-Vitamins. Joint manipulation and traction are effective treatments if there is pressure on the nerve. Massage is helpful if adhesions and tight muscles are compressing the nerve. Cold laser helps to speed recovery.

Traction Injuries
Traction injuries to the shoulder or neck can cause tingling, numbness and pain to the arms and fingers (as can disc herniations), and generally the PRICE routine is all you can do for a while, although cold laser may help speed recovery.

Nerve Compression and Irritation Injuries
Disc herniations, carpal tunnel syndrome, tarsal tunnel syndrome, piriformis syndrome, and thoracic outlet syndrome are all nerve compression and irritation injuries - with or without inflammation. Joint manipulation, massage, traction, and stretching are very effective treatments for these compression type injuries. These injuries are largely due to postural and biomechanical problems that repetitive motion finally triggered.

Neuropraxia, or crushing injuries to the nerves in your wrist, fingers, and toes are common from excessive jamming, tight shoes. Carpal tunnel and tarsal tunnel syndrome are due to compression of the nerves in your wrist and foot respectively – although other conditions like excessively tight muscles or footwear, or trigger points can mimic these syndromes. Protecting the area and waiting are the only truly successful treatments. Feeling can take months to come back. Hypothermia has a very similar prognosis. Traction, joint manipulation, Graston or Gua Sha, and rest are the treatment of choice.

Neurologic Issues Resulting From Genetic Abnormalities
Sometimes neurological problems are due to genetic abnormalities such as an extra cervical rib, beaked acromion, or spinal abnormalities which create extra pressure on nerves. It is a good idea to get several opinions from several specialists (orthopedists, chiropractors, physical therapists) to determine the best course of treatment as surgery may be the best or worst option.

SPINAL PROBLEMS

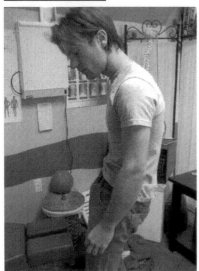

Poor Posture: Forward Head, Flat Back

Upper Cross Syndrome
Although not an injury itself, biomechanical (postural) problems can result in a whole host of symptoms and injuries from headaches, pain, numbness and tingling, to visceral problems. The most common postural problem experienced by climbers is known as "Upper Cross Syndrome". Symptoms can range from headaches, shoulder pain, neck pain, tingling and numbness in the hands or fingers, and mid back and shoulder blade pain. The postural problem consists of hypertonic tight chest, upper shoulder, and posterior neck muscles like the upper traps, lats, pecs, levator scapula, and sub-occipital muscles; weak and underdeveloped deep neck flexors and scapular stabilizers like the longus coli, lower traps, and serratus anterior. The cervical spine generally has a decreased to reversed cervical lordosis, and the thoracic spine has a hyperkyphosis in the upper section and a hypokyphosis in the lower (straight forward leaning neck, rounded upper back, and flat mid back). Students and computer users suffer similar postural problems, but constant belaying adds to the neck problems as well as overdeveloped pulling muscles with comparatively weak stabilizer muscles. Every inch your head is forward adds 10 pounds of stress to your back. Stretches, exercises, traction, cervical corrective pillows, and joint manipulation are key in correcting this postural problem.

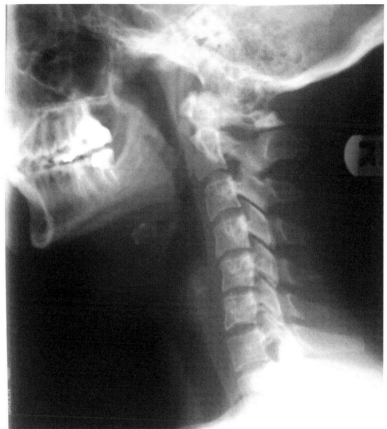

X-Ray of a Neck with a Reversed Cervical Curve:
Patient Complains of Headaches, Neck Pain, Shoulder Pain, and Tingling in Arms and Hands

Lower Cross Syndrome
Going in hand with upper cross syndrome is, you guessed it: Lower Cross Syndrome. People suffering from this can have low back pain, buttock pain, numbness and tingling in the butt (piriformis syndrome), legs (sciatica), or feet, hip pain, knee and foot pain. The cause is hypertonic and tight muscles – most commonly the hamstrings, hip flexors (illiopsoas), and piriformis. The weak muscles are generally the abdominals, intrinsic back muscles, gluteals, medial quads, and sometimes even the hamstrings (weak *and* tight). Structural issues arise from the lumbar spine and sacroiliac joints. The SI joint can be rotated, and the lumbar spine can either be hypolordotic (flat) or hyper lordotic (too much curve). Both structural curve problems can be caused from the same reason. Stretches, exercises (especially core exercises), and spinal manipulation are key components in rehabilitation.

Fixing your biomechanical problems in your spine will allow your muscles to function properly and reduce the chance of arthritis. Stretching and exercising your muscles will retrain your posture from slipping back into old habits. Ever get a massage that felt great but the next day you were back to square one? Ever see a chiropractor and felt good walking out the door but by the time you got home, you felt the same? Chances are you fit into the upper or lower cross syndrome category and need to hack away at the problem from all aspects. Light cardio, daily exercise, and stress reduction techniques will also help you from slipping back into old habits.

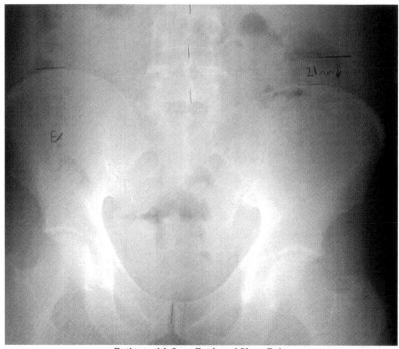

Patient with Low Back and Knee Pain
Right hip is 21mm lower than left. Left pelvis is externally rotated. L5 vertebra is rotated to the right.

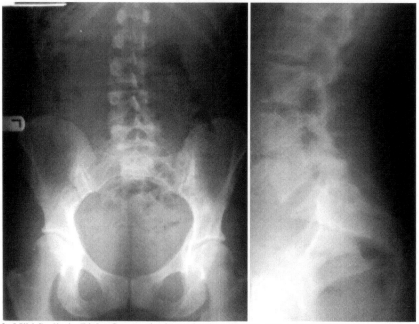

Left: Mild Scoliosis. Right: Sacrum is almost horizontal with film which puts stress on the L5 disc

FOOT PROBLEMS

Second only to your spine, your feet dictate how the biomechanics of your entire body will operate. Your body is one big kinetic chain, starting with your feet and ending with your head. Your feet need to pronate (roll from the outside of your heel on foot strike to the outside of your big toe or toe-off). To do this your foot needs to be flexible with normal arches.

Over-pronators have "floppy" feet with low or weak arches. Even if something is slightly off in your feet, you can experience symptoms anywhere up the line (the same is also true with your head and neck). Many health care practitioners will resort straight to orthotics, but really good practitioners (and it doesn't just have to be a podiatrist) will find correctable problems in your feet. Maybe your big toe doesn't flex enough? Maybe you have a leg length inequality? Maybe your talocrural joint is medially subluxated? Maybe you are wearing the wrong type of shoe? There are many things to look for, so spend your time and money wisely. Find an expert.

If you don't know where to look, start with a specialty running shop and go from there. Common foot problems include: over-pronation, hallux valgus, metatarsalgia, plantar fasciitis, bunions, calluses, ingrown toenails, blisters, and hammertoe.

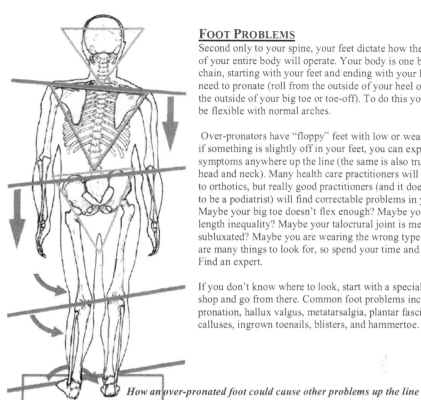

How an over-pronated foot could cause other problems up the line

Tibialis anterior
Extensor dig. longus
Ext. hall. long.
Ext. dig. brevis
Tendo calcaneus
Peronæus longus
Peronæus brevis
Peronæus tertius

FOOT AND ANKLE ANATOMY

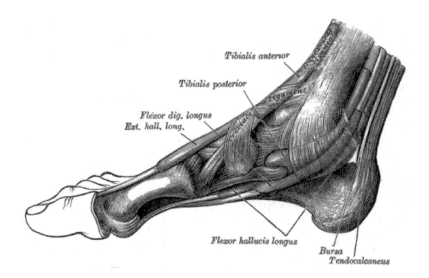

Tibialis anterior
Tibialis posterior
Flexor dig. longus
Ext. hall. long.
Flexor hallucis longus
Bursa
Tendocalcaneus

KNEE PROBLEMS

Luckily for climbers, knees are the least likely joint to be injured from overuse in climbing – but many climbers are runners, skiers, and hikers also, so they develop knee problems. The most common knee problems are patellar tracking issues due to overly tight hamstrings and weak medial quads (vastus medialis oblique or VMO), a leg length inequality, or a foot problem. Shin splints are generally due to foot problems, and ITB syndrome is usually caused by overly tight hamstrings or quads, a rotated pelvis or leg length inequality. Other knee problems climbers may suffer are runner's or jumper's knee, torn meniscus, LCL, MLC, ACL, or PCL, plicae syndrome, and chondromalacia patellae. Start by checking for foot disorders and improper footwear. Address muscle imbalances in your leg, thigh, and hips. Make sure your spine and pelvis are level and even. Meanwhile, address the area of pain in the knee itself by using some of the treatments outlined above. Nine times out of ten, the actually problem did not originate in the knee and it is a good idea to have someone besides you take a closer look.

SHOULDER PROBLEMS

Most shoulder problems are a result of a rotator cuff tear or labral tear (a labrum is like the meniscus in your knee). The shoulder is the sloppiest joint in the body, followed by the knee, then the ankle and wrist, which is a good thing, since it allows great freedom of movement, but it also allows for easy injury. Your rotator cuff is a collection of four muscles (supraspinatus, infraspinatus, teres minor, subscapularis) that provide stability and also keep your shoulder down and out of the joint. When the shoulder rides too high in the joint, the muscles (especially the supraspinatus) become impingened (or pinched) between your humerus and the acromion process on your scapula.

The most dangerous positions for your arms to be in are in an abducted (arms out to the side) and externally rotated position (like a field goal). Lateral raises and military presses are high risk exercises, and not very useful to be honest. Arm barring in offwidth climbing is an extremely high risk climbing position, as are full-on dyno. All these dangerous positions decrease the space for the muscles and tendons and place high stress on the smaller muscles and tendons. The goal in rehab, once the inflammation is reduced, is to position your shoulder blades (scapula) down and back and your neck retracted (see upper cross syndrome). This creates a stable shoulder and increases the space in your shoulder joint. Aggressive rehab is critical for preventing this from becoming a lifelong problem.

Treatment for chronically dislocating shoulders is a total re-strengthening of the shoulder complex, including stretching overly tight muscles. Surgery and prolotherapy are options for both if rehab fails. Frozen shoulder is when your body clamps down on your shoulder joint, causing pain and immobility. Aggressive treatment is NOT recommended as it can make the shoulder more irritated and cause further immobility. Cold laser, cross-friction, Graston/Gua Sha, massage, gentle joint manipulation (of the shoulder, scapula, collar-bone, mid back, and neck), electrical-stimulation and ultrasound combo, prolotherapy, and bracing are all effective treatments.

Shoulder (Anterior View) Anatomy

Note Space Between Acromion and Humerus for Structures to Become Impinged.

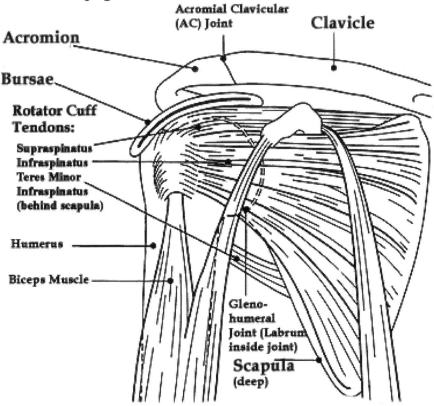

Acromial Clavicular (AC) Joint

Clavicle

Acromion

Bursae

Rotator Cuff Tendons:

Supraspinatus
Infraspinatus
Teres Minor
Infraspinatus
(behind scapula)

Humerus

Biceps Muscle

Gleno-
humeral
Joint (Labrum
inside joint)

Scapula
(deep)

ELBOW PROBLEMS

Elbow problems are common for climbers. Lateral epicondylitis ranks in as the top elbow injury and is addressed in tendonitis section. Medial Epicondylitis is more commonly a sprain/strain acute type injury although it can become reoccurring. Addressing muscle imbalances, changing your form and technique, bracing in the meantime, joint manipulation, and massage are the best options. Prolotherapy is a good option when these other treatments fail.

WRIST INJURIES

These are also quite common. Bracing, joint manipulation, cross-friction, traction, Graston and Gua Sha, are all good treatments. The most common wrist injury is a general wrist or thumb sprain/strain followed by broken bones. Rest and immobilization followed by joint manipulation are the treatments of choice. Prolotherapy is an effective treatment for chronically loose painful snapping wrists.

Your wrist has a structure similar to your knee meniscus or shoulder labrum called the triangular fibrocartilage located in the wrist below ringer and little finger. Injury to this sometimes requires surgery, or a lot of rest and rehab since it has no immediate blood supply. Symptoms are chronic, recurring pain in the area sometimes followed with snapping or popping. Rest, taping/bracing, and cold laser are the best non-invasive treatments. Another common, but serious wrist injury is a fracture of the scaphoid bone, located just below your thumb. Part of the bone has no blood supply, so if broken off from the rest of the bone, the piece will die causing serious complication. Always get a wrist x-ray if you suspect that your wrist is broken.

FINGER PROBLEMS

The best thing to do to prevent nasty finger (pulley) sprains and tears is to not overdo crimps and one and two finger pockets. The muscles in your hand and forearm must be strong enough to support the huge stresses placed on your fingers (the same goes with all joints – which is why you can be so sore when beginning a new weight training or running program and more susceptible to injury when learning a new sport). The tendons and ligaments take much longer to toughen up than your muscles do. The goal is to slowly increase your finger training exercises and limit climbs with excessive finger strain. If you do a finger intense climb, round out your day with juggier routes to give your fingers a break. A proper warm-up is crucial. Tape your fingers if you plan on working a finger-intensive route. If you are going to climb hard and train hard, your odds of rupturing a finger pulley or tearing a rotator cuff or labrum is very high – so be prepared. Get health insurance! Bracing, cross-friction, Graston and Gua Sha, cold laser, ultrasound, and prolotherapy are good treatments.

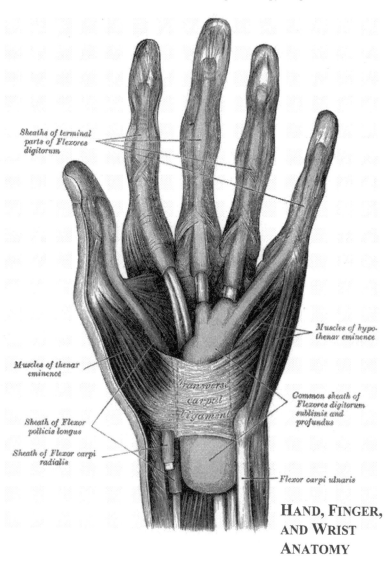

Sheaths of terminal parts of Flexores digitorum

Muscles of hypo-thenar eminence

Muscles of thenar eminence

Transverse carpal ligament

Common sheath of Flexores digitorum sublimis and profundus

Sheath of Flexor pollicis longus

Sheath of Flexor carpi radialis

Flexor carpi ulnaris

HAND, FINGER, AND WRIST ANATOMY

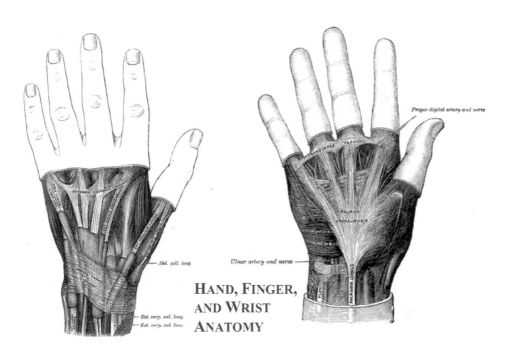

Proper digital artery and nerve

Abd. poll. long.

Ulnar artery and nerve

Ext. carp. rad. long.
Ext. carp. rad. brev.

Hand, Finger, and Wrist Anatomy

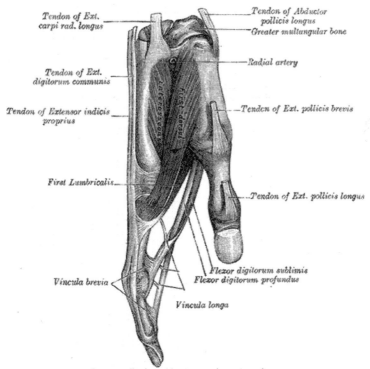

Tendon of Ext. carpi rad. longus

Tendon of Abductor pollicis longus

Greater multangular bone

Radial artery

Tendon of Ext. digitorum communis

Tendon of Extensor indicis proprius

Tendon of Ext. pollicis brevis

First Lumbricalis

Tendon of Ext. pollicis longus

Flexor digitorum sublimis
Flexor digitorum profundus

Vincula brevia

Vincula longa

Rehabilitation Through Exercise

I have included some exercises for rehabbing various body areas pulling from the previous exercises and have included a few extras that are specific to rehab. Of course they are not all-inclusive. For example, if you're recovering from an Achilles tendon rupture, the foot and ankle rehab will help, but you'll need some more specific exercises as well, and you'll want to avoid some of the exercises to prevent re-injury.

I've tried to cover stretches for the most commonly tight muscles and exercises for the most commonly weak muscles for a particular area. Like I mentioned earlier, cookbook treatments don't work - so don't follow the exercises like one. If a stretch feels ineffective, it probably is. If it's tight – stretch it. If it's weak – exercise it. If it hurts – STOP and re-evaluate. For example, if you are experiencing low back pain, the exercises that extended you spine may aggravate your condition. The same may be true for the exercises that flex your back.

Generally speaking, the exercises listed below begin with acute rehab and stretches, and progress to more demanding functional exercises. Your injured area may not be ready for all the exercises listed, so skip the ones that hurt. You should start with pain free active range of motion and stretching, then progress to rubber tubing, then to body weight exercises, then to weights, and finally add a proprioceptive element (like doing the exercise on a wobble board). Not every photo shows the tubing version, body weight version, weighted version, and proprioceptive version - so you have to be creative. Specific injures require specific exercises and likewise, some injuries require NOT performing a specific movement. When in doubt, always consult with an expert in a particular injury.

Light pain free movement
Your heart doesn't pump blood from muscles, organs, and other tissues into your veins, but muscular contractions do. If you can move an area without causing further injury, movement will help decrease swelling, and as an added benefit, will give you a major head start on rehab by keeping your muscles firing and active.

Stretching
This is covered in great detail earlier in the book. Once again, don't overstretch an area. Meet the resistance of the area, and hold it. Gradually increase the stretch in a pain free range of motion.

Weights, Tubing, Body Weight
To strengthen an injured area, you first need to make sure it has healed enough to weight bear, and then stretched first if it was overly tight. Begin rehab using light tubing, progressing steadily using stronger and stronger bands. Now you are ready for body weight functional exercises. These are the most effective because they mimic the function of your injured area. After you are able to support body weight, it's time to add weight to strengthen the area to meet the needs of your desired activity. Don't over do it because you're going to have to start all over if you re-injure the area!

****

Neck and Thoracic Rehab

These stretches and exercises are meant to re-train your neck and uppe.
They will help with neck pain, headaches, and mid-back pain.

Acute Phase Exercises and Stretches

Perform the following stretches from the Stretching section:
Whole Body Stretches (all), Neck Stretches, Rhomboid Stretch, Posterior Cap
Stretch, Pec Corner Stretch, and Neck Pillow or orthodic stretch (see braces an
section for more information)

Perform the following exercises from the Core Exercises section:
Wall or Ground Angels, Chin Retraction.

Post-Acute Phase Rehab (do these exercises when you are out of the pain stage)

Perform the following exercise from the Core Exercises section:
Isometric Deep Neck Flexors

Perform the following <u>new</u> exercise:
Head Weights
If you can locate a set (online, or at a chiropractic clinic that specializes in cervical correction), these weights re-train your neck muscles to pull your head back into the correct position over your shoulders. By placing 2-8 lbs on your forehead, you will instinctively pull your head back to neutral. To avoid slowly sagging forward, sit on a ball or wobble disc and actively move your pelvis. Five to twenty minutes every other day to twice a day will provide the time needed to make a change.

Low Back Rehab

These stretches and exercises help with low back pain, sciatica, and resultant symptoms for "lower cross" syndrome. Don't be alarmed at the lack of new exercises in this section, nothing has been left out.

Acute Phase Exercises and Stretches

Perform the following stretches from the Stretching section:
Piriformis Stretch, Psoas Stretch, Hamstring Stretch, Lumbar Stretches (all)

Perform the following exercises from the Core Exercises section:
Pelvic Tilts Track

Post Acute Phase Rehab (do these exercises when you are out of the pain stage)

Perform the following exercises from the Core Exercises section:
Lumbar Core Stability Tracks (all exercises in progression). Start with the simplest exercises and progress slowly. Perfecting the easiest exercises is more important.

ANKLE REHAB

...s and exercises are meant to re-train your foot and ankle to maintain your arch support, and ...nt mechanics, including pronation during gait. These will also help with lower leg, and knee issues.

ACUTE PHASE EXERCISES AND STRETCHES

Perform the following stretch from the Stretching section:
Calf Stretch (see stretching section)

Perform the following <u>new</u> stretches:
Tibialis Anterior Stretch
Basically the opposite of the calf stretch.

Hallux Valgus Stretch
Put your thumb at the head of the 1st metatarsal (on the outside of the base of your big toe) and your index finger in the inside of the tip of your big toe. Push with your thumb and resist with your index finger as your try to squeeze your big toe inwards.

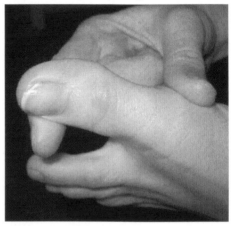

Plantar Fascia Stretch
Pull your toes back with your heel on the ground.

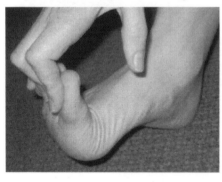

Plantar Fascia Massage
Using a bottle (try a cold one out of the fridge), roll it back and forth on the bottom of your foot. For more pinpoint massage, use a golf ball.

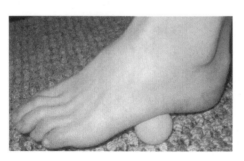

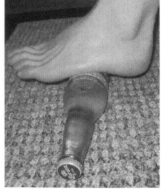

118

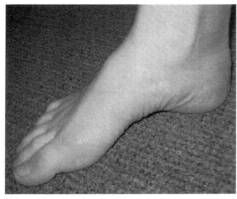

Perform the following <u>new</u> exercises
Short Foot
While sitting, try to make the arch in your foot bigger without curling your toes – thus shortening your foot. Start by passively molding your foot to get the idea, then try it without help. Next try it weight bearing. Use short foot position in all exercises and activities possible if you suffer from weak or flattened arches.

Alphabet
Using your big toe as a stylus, write the alphabet in the air. Make capitol letters, lower case, and cursive to get the full range of motion.

REHAB PHASE POST ACUTE EXERCISES (do these exercises when you are out of the pain stage)
Perform the following <u>new</u> exercises:
Toe Abduction
Put a rubber band around your toes and try to spread them.

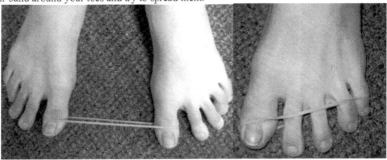

Toe Adduction
Using cork, or earplugs and squeeze your toes together.

Marble Grab
Try and pick up various sized objects such as marbles with your toes.

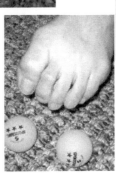

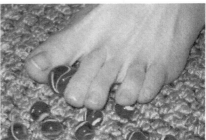

Towel Curl
Lay a towel flat out on the ground. Using your toes, squinch the towel up towards you. To make it harder, put a weight on the end of the towel.

One Leg Stand
Use a chair for support if difficult. Close your eyes to make it more difficult.

Ankle Dorsiflexion
Start by using a Thera-Band around your toes. Next walk around on your heels until it burns. You can put a dumbbell under your toes and lift it repeatedly for strength training.

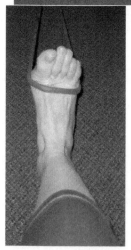

Ankle Plantar Flexion (Toe Raises)
Start with light tubing and flex your ankle. Progress to a double leg toe or calf raise. Finally try it with one leg.

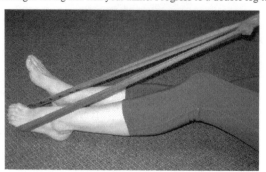

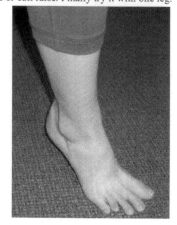

Ankle Inversion

Put tubing around the arch of your foot and turn your whole foot (avoid pointing your toes or rotating your knee) inward.

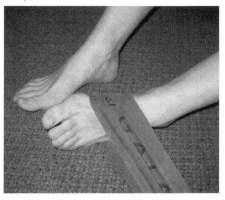

Ankle Eversion

As above but turn your foot outward.

Wobble Board Stand

There are many ways to progress, but the idea is to start with both feet on an unstable surface and progress to a one leg stand on the most unstable surface possible. The ideal starting surface is a pillow, progressing to a rocker board or ½ of a foam roller (a rocker board rocks front to back only), to a wobble board or vestibular disc. You can cut a firm ball in half and glue it to the bottom of a pair of sandals for a great final challenge.

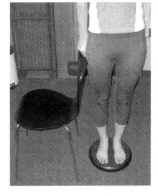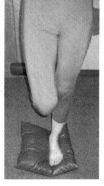

Sit to Stand on a Wobble Board

Sit on the edge of a firm surface with a wobble board or disc under your feet. Not without using your arms, slowly stand onto the unstable surface.

KNEE REHAB

If in doubt of the weak link, go over the foot rehab exercises also. These exercises help correct common muscle imbalances in your knee and hip (especially the VMO) which lead to patellar tracking issues. I have included some very basic exercises for those rehabbing a post-surgical knee.

ACUTE PHASE EXERCISES AND STRETCHES

Perform the following stretches from the stretching section:
Leg/Hip Stretches (all)

Perform the following exercises from the Core Exercises section
Side Lying and Side Bridge Track

Perform the following <u>new</u> exercises:

Terminal Knee Extension
Sitting with a towel or pillow under the affected knee, or later in rehab sitting or standing with rubber tubing, start with your knee slightly bent and press your knee down into the towel or against the tubing by squeezing your thigh muscle.

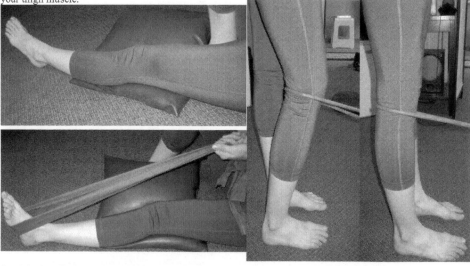

Straight Leg Raise
Lying on your back with your legs straight, gently raise your entire leg with your foot turned slightly outward.

Toe Raises

Standing on just your affected leg with a chair for support, raise yourself up onto your toes.

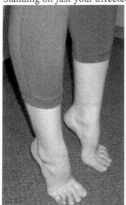

Knee Extension

Sitting in a chair with your feet on the floor, gently raise your leg, squeezing your quad/thigh muscle. Hold, lower, and repeat. Attach tubing to your ankle and behind the chair for resistance.

Hamstring Curls

Lay on your stomach with tubing tied around the ankle of the affected leg and attached to an anchor at floor level. Slowly pull your heel towards you buttocks while pointing your toes. Progress to a weight machine much later in your rehab.

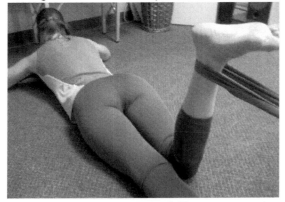

Step-up and Step-down

These exercises require a stable surface such as a stool or a box slightly lower than the height of your knee. Place the foot of the involved leg on the stool, and with control, raise the opposite foot onto the stool. Avoid leaning your upper body forward and do not "push off" with your back foot. Lower the uninvolved foot back down and repeat. After you are able to do this, try stepping down with the involved leg first. Now stand alongside the stool and repeat the previous exercises sideways.

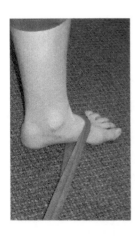

External Hip Rotation

Lay on your side with legs extended and stacked on top of each other. Raise your top, affected leg up slightly. Externally rotate your entire affected raised leg until your toe points to the ceiling and the rotate it back.

Internal Rotation

Begin seated. Attach tubing to the middle of the foot of the affected leg and to an anchor at floor level. Keep the foot flat on the floor and pull the tubing inward by rotating the lower leg. Keep the knee bent at 90 degrees and centered over the ankle at all times. Now try the exercise standing (the knee is now at 180 degrees during movement).

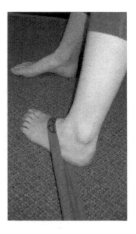

POST ACUTE PHASE REHAB (do these exercises when you are out of the pain stage)
Perform the following exercises from the Lower Body Weight Training section:
Wall Squats, Squats and Lunges (begin with no weight), Leg Press and Hamstring Curls, Calf Raises

Perform the following exercises from the Core Exercises section: Bridge Track

Perform the following <u>new</u> exercises
Backward Lunge

Step backward with the affected leg keeping your body upright, and slowly lower your body down until the back knee almost touches the floor. The front knee should not bend past 90 degrees. With control, step forward to return to the starting position.

One leg Squats (see "one leg squats" under the lower body weight training section)
Start with quarter squats before progressing further. You can add a heel raise at the top to increase the effectiveness of the exercise. For greater functionality, perform these next on a rocker board or ½ of a foam roller, wobble board, or balance sandals. Use a chair for support if needed.

Hops

Begin with small hops using both legs. Jump forwards and backwards, then side to side. Next try standing on just one leg. If you have access, tie heavy tubing or bungee cord around your waist for resistance.

124

Ball Catch

Standing on a rocker board, ½ a foam roller, wobble board, or other unstable surface of choice, toss a medicine ball back and forth with a partner. Your knees should be bent at about 45 degrees. Now try it standing on just one leg.

SHOULDER REHAB

These stretches and exercises are designed to rehab a post-surgical shoulder, or for those suffering from impingement syndrome or a chronically dislocating shoulder.

ACUTE PHASE STRETCHES AND EXERCISES

Perform the following stretches from the Stretching section:
Shoulder Stretches (all)

Perform the following exercises from the Upper Body Weight Training and Core sections:
Triceps Exercises, Rows, Prone Plank Track (all).

Find weak links by trying exercises in the neck or thoracic stretches and exercises in the Injury Section. Do not take this suggestion lightly; it could be the key to fixing your shoulder problem!

Perform the following <u>new</u> exercises:
Shoulder Pendulum

Stand or kneel bent over with the affected arm dangling limp. Using slight momentum from your torso, make your flaccid arm swing back and forth like a pendulum. Do not use any arm or shoulder muscles to help. Experiment by making small and large circles in opposite directions, figure 8's, and back and forth motions. When tolerable, lightly grip a small 1-3 pound weight or soup can. Progress to 8-10 lbs or use a milk jug.

Wall Walk
Stand arms width away from the wall. Walk your fingers up the wall in front of you as far as comfortable. Now do it laterally (sideways – shown on right photo). Avoid shrugging your shoulder.

POST ACUTE PHASE REHAB (do these exercises when you are out of the pain stage)
Perform the following exercises from the Core Exercises section:
All shoulder core exercises

Perform the following <u>new</u> exercises:
Scaption
Standing, bring the affected arm to 30 degrees in front of your body and turn your thumb up. Now raise the arm to shoulder level, keeping the arm straight. Stand tall and keep the shoulder blade down and back throughout the motion. Hold and repeat.

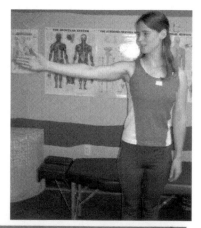

Side-lying Internal Rotation
The reason this exercise was not included in the generic shoulder core exercises is that this muscle is generally overdeveloped in climbers in relation to the external rotators. If injured, this is the exercise to rehab it. Lay on your side with the affected arm on the floor and at a 90/90 degree position and holding a small weight. Internally rotating your arm, lift the weight off the floor until it is perpendicular to the floor.

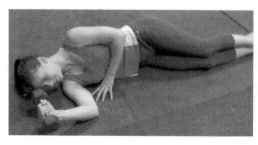 

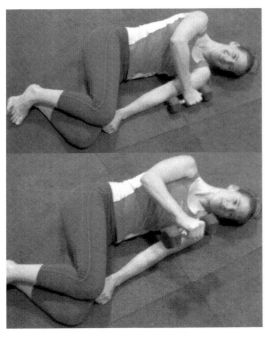

Side-lying External Rotation
Lying on your side with the side you want to work up, externally rotate your arm to 90 degrees. Keep your elbow tucked in your side. Use very light weight and do no over-do this exercise as it can lead to shoulder injury.

Side-lying Abduction
Same as above but raise your arm towards the ceiling only 30 degrees. Keep your shoulders down. Use very light weight and do no over-do this exercise as it can lead to shoulder injury.

Prone Scapular Retraction

The next exercises are all similar, so this will be described in greatest detail. Begin lying face down on a weight bench with the affected arm hanging down towards the floor, and holding a light amount of weight (0-10 lbs). This exercise requires weight in both arms, the others do not. Squeeze your shoulder blades together and down, squeezing through the mid back.

Prone Shoulder Extension

Place affected arm alongside your body with the thumb pointed down. Raise your straightened arm up backwards.

Prone Shoulder Abduction

Raise your straightened arm up to shoulder level to assume a 'T' position.

ELBOW AND FOREARM REHAB

Since almost all of the muscles in your elbow and forearm are located between your shoulder and your wrist, all of the exercises have already be covered. Below is an all-around elbow rehab routine to work the supporting musculature that have been most likely overwhelmed by your enormous biceps and finger flexors – most commonly resulting in Lateral Epicondylitis.

ACUTE PHASE STRETCHES AND EXERCISES
Perform the following stretches and exercises from the Stretching , Wrist Core, and Finger and Wrist Rehab sections:
Finger and Wrist Stretches (all), Wrist Core (all), Putty Squeeze (wrist or finger flexor rehab only – not for Lateral Epicondylitis!)

POST ACUTE PHASE REHAB (do these exercises when out of the Pain Stage)
Perform the following exercises from the Upper Body Weight Training section:
Triceps Curl, One Arm Pull-Down, Hammer Swing.
For rehabbing strained wrist and finger flexors only – not for Lateral Epicondylitis: Biceps Curl, Pull-Ups, Finger Curls, Wrist Curls, Farmers Carry, Weighted Dowel Roll.

FINGER AND WRIST REHAB

These exercises will help those recovering from blown finger pulleys, wrist surgery, and carpal tunnel syndrome.

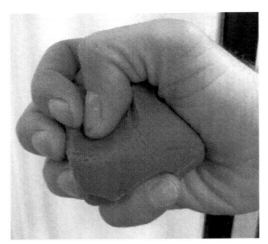

ACUTE PHASE STRETCHES AND EXERCISES
Perform the following stretches from the Stretching section:
Wrist and Finger Stretches (all), Whole Arm Doorway and Wall Stretch

Perform the following <u>new</u> exercises:
Alphabet with Wrist
Rest your forearm on a table or your leg and make a fist. Move your wrist, pretending to trace the alphabet –exactly like described in the ankle alphabet exercise.
Putty Squeeze
Either buy commercial hand putty, or find something with resistance like a soft rubber ball. Squeeze and work the putty.

POST ACUTE PHASE REHAB (do these exercises when you are out of the pain stage)
Perform the following exercises from the Upper Body Weight Training and Core Exercise sections:
Wrist Core (all exercises), Finger Curls, Wrist Curls, Weighted Dowel Roll, Farmers Cary

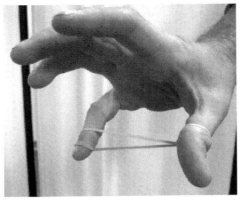

Perform the following <u>new</u> exercises:
Single Finger Abduction and Extension
Instead of all your fingers, just spread two fingers open and apart connected by a rubber band.

CHAPTER THREE: NUTRITION

Southwest British Columbia

This section will help you decide what and how much to eat and drink on your climb. For the best book on eating well, read Eat, Drink, and Be Healthy, by Walter Willett. To keep your energy reserves high, you need to at least put in what you're burning. This means that you need to up your caloric intake while climbing or approaching. This is not intended to be a weight loss program, so don't treat it as one. In order to balance how much you can carry to move quickly and how much you actually need to eat without going into caloric debt, **two pounds of food per person per day** is a good weight to shoot for.

Pack all your food free floating in the dead spaces of your pack for the hike in, and have today's lunch in a zip lock or in your pockets. Put stuff like Ziplocs of cocoa and packets of oatmeal in a grocery store plastic bag. That will save them from tearing, and you can use the bag to hang your food at camp since it weighs less than a stuff sack. Your first empty zip lock will become your garbage bag.

SUGGESTED EATING
Breakfast
Breakfast is a Catch-22. It's the most important meal of the day, but you want to make it quick unless you've got time to kill. Items such as instant hot cereals and oatmeal prepare quickly. Precooking a hard boiled egg or two makes a quick breakfast and is a little more long-lasting than instant oatmeal – but it is heavier. Instant food is nice, but the nutritional value is terrible. Instant oatmeal has little value except that it's hot and easy to make. You might as well just eat a couple energy bars instead and save your stove fuel for your drink. Try and get organic instant oatmeal to get the most out of it. Add some dried blueberries and powdered nog to add some flavor and texture.

Hot chocolate is a lot less dehydrating and has more energy than coffee, as is instant chai. Make it mocha chai or cocoa with some instant coffee if you need that caffeine. Starbucks has a new instant coffee that is worth trying. Jell-o makes a great hot drink. Tea doesn't really seem to be worth the effort since it has no calories. Tea is a better for a drink for dinner unless habit requires you to have it. No hot drink is the quickest and lightest option. Chug some water, cough down a bar and go!

Lunch
Bring lots of little quick tasty snacks with sugar and fat. If you actually enjoy energy bars, go for it. There are some pretty good bars out there, but I've found that if you eat them constantly you're going to never want to eat them again! Power-Bars always seem to provide more energy than they should, although you need to choke them down with lots of water, and they are too hard to eat in the winter. A new favorite are the RAW Revolution bars. Sounds gross? They are actually just crushed nuts, dates, and are really oily. If you skip on the bars, just bring a couple for the bottom of your pack in case you need them in an emergency. Candy bars are an acceptable substitute if they don't melt. Check candy bar wrappers for calories. Also, be aware of what food won't melt in the summer, and break your teeth in the winter. When exercising, you don't want to consume much protein because you want your energy immediately available. Check your lunch items for protein content. Bars and snacks high in protein may be best left for after dinner snacks. The simple sugars in candy, sucrose (table sugar) and high fructose corn-syrup don't give you as much energy as quality energy bars will and lead to the inevitable sugar crash due to the insulin rebound. However, I find that if you aren't sitting around and constantly moving, then usually the crash can be avoided.

For pure carbs, Gu and Cliffshot are great if you actually eat one packet every 15-30 minutes and can afford that. Hammergel is a bit more affordable than Gu and comes in big bottles. Brown rice syrup mixed with chocolate sauce is gross, but works for those on a serious budget. I jokingly suggested bringing a bottle of Corn Syrup instead of Gu on a climb once. My partner followed through with the idea, and although he had plenty of energy, he was sick to his stomach most of the climb. There are "energy" gummies out there (Sharkies, Cliff Blocks, and Jelly-Belly Energy Beans) and I for one am hooked. They are a lot less messy than gels, and easier to ration. Gummy bears, fruit snacks, and Swedish Fish will do in a pinch, but they don't have as many complex carbohydrates as the energy gummies. I like to buy a bag of mixed taffy and stash some in my pockets to eat while I'm approaching for a little sugar and something to keep my mind off slogging.

*Try **making your own gummies**. Here's my recipe: In a saucepan, bring to a slow boil: 10oz Knox gelatin, 12oz Jell-o, 1 cup sugar (use your favorite sports drink mix as a substitute), 2 cups brown rice syrup, salt, 4 tbs. olive oil (or flax seed oil), and 4 cups juice (Bolthouse Farms, Naked, or Odwalla green and or blue fruits/veggie work well). Be creative! Add a couple packets of electrolyte mix, a couple little bottles of 5-Hour Energy Drink, extra salt, vitamins (careful of making it taste yucky), protein powder, powdered greens, etc. If you can figure out the proportions, substitute the Jell-o for the same amount of unflavored gelatin and fill in the sugar with your drink mix. You may also want to try adding less gelatin if the finished product will hold together. Brown rice syrup solids and carnauba wax are better substitutes for the Jell-o but are hard to find and expensive. Pour the mixture into a pan coated with olive oil spray, and put it in the fridge for a few hours. Cut the finished product into little squares and put them into tiny zip-locks to store in your fridge or freezer.*

*Make **"Trail-mix Krispie Treats"** by substituting your favorite trail mix, nuts, fruit, and /granola for Rice Krispies in a Rice Krispie Treat recipe to make your own version of an energy bar. Add honey and/or brown rice syrup to take the place of some or all of the marshmallows.*

*I like to puree fruits and vegetables and make **fruit and veggie roll-ups** on longer trips to satisfy my fruits and veggie deficiencies. All you do is pour the puree onto a cookie sheet in a thin layer, and bake at 150 degrees with the oven door open for a few hours. I coat everything with olive oil spray to keep it from sticking. With a few of your homemade trail mix bars, shot blocks, and fruit roll-ups (with some meat snacks tossed in) you can take care of breakfast and lunch for your trip without breaking the bank on store bought bars and gels.*

One can never have enough fatty snacks unless your climb requires constant movement – then just bring a few because you will have a hard time digesting them. I discovered the joy of instant pre-cooked bacon strips and never leave home without them. They are full of nitrates, but you should be worried about fat and calories, not long term cancer. If you must, make your own bacon ahead of time, but it's nowhere near as good. Other good meat snacks are beef, turkey, salmon, deer, or soy jerky, landjeager, pepperoni, and salami (Sopresetta salami has the most fat). I sometimes use the travel size cream cheese packets as my Gu shots in times of financial hardship, and smoked salmon in times of financial gain.

The "MEATON" Found in an actual bag of beef jerky.
Justin Thibault photo.

Bread products like bagels take up space and don't have many calories, but they are nice sometimes to fill the gut. Cheese is always good, and they make little pre-wrapped cheddar packets. Chewy granola bars are like a hybrid bread product/candy bar. Companies are making some very yummy yogurt iced bars, and salty & sweet trail mix bars. A cheap and easy snack is a simple baked potato, or hard-boiled egg. No packaging necessary

Bacon in the Picket Range, Washington
Eric Wolfe Photo

It's nice to have some dried fruit to round out your diet. Costco sells the most amazing dried mango you'll ever eat. Mangos and apricots are also very high in potassium. Pack your lunch so you can eat something at any time throughout the climb. Trail mixes don't work as well because they are hard to get at when belaying or climbing and spill all over. Those little 99 cent packets of nuts are a lot easier to eat on the go. While packing, lay out one of each type of snack out in little piles for each day until it looks like you have enough.

If you're not going fast and light, the best lunch is a simple bread or bagel sandwich loaded with your favorite lunch meat and cheese, some nuts, an apple, some cheese, and a candy bar. I use cream cheese as my sandwich spread to up the calories a bit. Plus it tastes awesome.

Dinner

Dinner is the meal where you want to fill up on fat, a moderate amount of protein, and still plenty of carbs. The main dish should be carbohydrate based, garnished with a generous helping of protein and fat. Most freeze dried meals only have the carb portion taken care of. Olive oil is a great source of fat calories, so bring a small bottle and drench your food in it. Foil pouches of tuna fish (or flavored tuna steaks) are excellent additions to a dinner to get your protein and oils (if the tuna is packed in oil versus water). The more you eat for dinner, the more energy you will have the next day and the warmer you will sleep.

> *Four night dinner menu.*
> *Dinner One: Mashed potato flakes. Add olive oil, smoked salmon or tuna, and cheese. Add Taco Bell hot-sauce packets, or Dairy Queen Tabasco packets you grabbed on the drive for flavor.*
> *Dinner Two: Freeze dried meal. Make sure it's the kind without tons of packaging. Check the calories. Lots of freeze dried dinners don't provide many calories! Add some cheese, olive oil, and some salami.*
> *Dinner Three: Couscous, tuna, olive oil and cheese.*
> *Dinner Four: Noodle Soup mix, salami, and cheese.*

Whole grains are a lot more nutritious than things made with white flour or potatoes, so if you can, try and find good whole grains that are quick to prepare. Check in the health section of the market to see if they have whole grain oatmeal, and dinner grains that prepare quickly.

Try Miso soup packets for your hot drink. They are not only delicious, but provide extra salt and protein. Ramen is filling and delicious but not the most nutritious soup out there. For dessert have an energy bar. Better yet, to get more fats eat a halva bar, and or trail mix and nuts for dessert. Mark Twight suggests Nuttella, a chocolate spread made with hazelnuts. If you really want to anger your partner, foil wrap a 16oz filet mignon with garlic mashed potatoes you bought at the Outback Steakhouse the day before for one of your dinners. A climbing partner of mine brought a rotisserie chicken on an alpine ice climb (and thus named the route Alpine Chicken). Remember: unless you need to be ultra light and movin' fast, it won't slow you down to bring some good food.

"I'm Lovin' It!" North Cascades, WA

Alcohol

I do not recommend bringing alcohol with you! But if you do, here are some tips. Nothing beats a beer at camp the first night or the night after the climb if you can manage the weight. A light Platypus water container can be filled with all sorts of hard stuff. You'll be glad you brought it if the weather sucks. Fill a Nalgene with Sake, and heat it in the pan while you boil your water for dinner. In Alaska I filled one Nalgene up with rum and the other with pina colada mix and was quite popular on storm days. Some genius came up with the idea of a Gatorade margarita: just mix lemon-lime Gatorade powder with tequila!

HYDRATION

Mt. Baker, WA

I sometimes bring powdered lemonade or a quality sports drink, like Accelerade, to make a drink at a rest break in my one-liter pot. I don't like to put mix in my water bladder or bottles because I inevitably just want plain water and it makes the container nasty for later. If I stop by a stream I'll pull out my cup or pot and make a flavored drink then and there. If you bring two Nalgene-type bottles, then just fill one with mix. I only go all out with a carb loaded water bladder if the climb requires an all-day and into the night exertion.

Mt. Stuart, WA

In the winter I keep one freshly boiled water bottle in my pack and one luke-warm bottle in an insulated water bottle holder (Outdoor Research makes good ones) at my hip. I only use hard plastic Nalgenes in the winter. For one, the plastic causes health problems (but I can deal for the few days a year I put them to use), and I inevitably lose them in the summer. Empty sports drink one liter bottles work just fine and are easy to rig to clip on your harness.

During exercise keep hydrated. **To stay hydrated you need a little less than one liter of water for every two hours of exercise. One liter of water weights 2.2 pounds.** So for a 9 hour day you'd need to drink 4.5 liters which would weigh 10 pounds! Is this possible? Obviously not, so drink it up at camp, and if you know you'll pass by a water source, try and fill up.

To drink this much water you need to maintain your electrolytes. Electrolyte replacement tablets are available that don't contain sugar and are flavored (Nuun makes a good one). I've found that these tablets keep my energy levels high and my recovery time low, especially in hot weather. Twin Labs makes a small spray-bottle if you don't like spiking your water.

You can also add a 6% carb drink mix to your water, maltodextrin being the best type of carb to add. This roughly equals 60g, 2oz, or 6 level tablespoons of carbohydrate powder per liter which is equivalent to 220kCal per liter. You can even try adding 2% protein powder to your water in addition to the carbs for enhanced recovery (Accelerade makes their mix in this ratio).

2% protein per liter roughly equals 20g, 0.7oz, or one level tablespoon of protein powder per liter and is equivalent to 80kCal per liter. **A 4:1 carb to protein drink mix of 6 Tbs carbs and 1 tbs protein will yield 300kCal per liter.** If you're drinking enough water you'll be getting 150kCal per hour from your water.

I must add that water in this dose of carbs and protein can get kinda gross – so don't leave it out for a long time. Also, you may get cottonmouth from the thicker water. If this is the case carry a container of pure water, or get your calories another way. Also, do not attempt to mix drink mix with electrolyte mix without first matching flavors, and testing it before your trip. I can attest that orange Accelerade at full concentration does not mix well with two tablets of cola Nuun no matter how physiologically beneficial it may seem. I now carry a strong drink mix water bottle and an electrolyte water bottle (which helps to wash out the thick feeling in your mouth) separately on my harness or running belt.

Example: If your water bladder holds 3 liters of water, you'd need to add 18 tablespoons of carb powder and 3 tablespoons of protein power. This will give you 900 calories worth of energy and should last you six hours. If your climb is 9 hours total car to car you'd need 4.5 liters of water and you'd get 1350 calories from just your water alone!

COUNTING CALORIES

How many calories do you need for a climb? To start you need to know how many calories you burn doing nothing at all (your resting metabolic rate). Kilocalories are the same thing as "calories" on nutrition labels. This equation will tell you your resting metabolic rate (how much you burn watching soap operas)

66.5 + (13.75 * your weight in Kg) + (5 * your height in cm) – (6.78 * your age in years) = resting metabolic rate (RMR). 1 pound = 0.454 Kg and 1 inch = 2.53cm.

Next you're going to need to know how much energy you spend extra besides just existing! This equation will tell you:

RMR + 600kCal per hour of intense exercise (i.e. every hour you spend training or actually climbing – factor in down time) = kilocalories need to eat for that 24 hour period.

Your totals will be alarmingly high (see the example below) and the answers to these equations are definitely on the high estimate side of things. It really isn't possible to pack that much food and water, lest take the time to eat and digest that! However, it's clear that you're going to need to eat a lot and this might clue you in as to why you got tired on your last climb and felt terrible the next day.

Carbs should equal 60-70% of your total intake, fat 20-25%, and protein 12-20%.

Fat = 220kcal per ounce. Protein and Carbs = 97kcal per ounce.

If you're spicing up your water with the 4:1 carb/protein drink mix from the hydration section, **subtract the drink mix calories from the solid food carb and protein calories, and re-calculate to find out how much food to bring.** You basically need a pound less of food!

To fix this problem of how much you should eat vs. how much you can carry, you're going to want to carb load. Load up a few days before the climb so you've got reserve stores of energy on the climb. Be sure to have lots of snacks (and beer) in the car and some money to eat big on the way home! If you're on an expedition, make sure you've got a ridiculous amount of high calorie comfort food to graze on all day at camp. Chug a ton of water in the morning, and try and re-fill your water on the approach or the climb if possible.

CARB LOADING

This is the best solution to get those extra calories in without having your backpack weight too much. The rule of thumb is to **eat 4.7g of carbs per day per pound of body weight for three to four days prior**. Knowing that there are **4 calories in one gram of carbs**, we can figure out how many carb calories to eat.

Eating this amount in cooked pasta is roughly 1.25 full packages of spaghetti a day. Not only is this a lot to eat, but it can totally clog up your digestive track – and make you have to poop a lot on your climb! Instead of the traditional spaghetti diet, make up these carb calories in highly concentrated drink mixes and bulk energy gel (such as Hammergel). The carbs should be roughly 70% of your diet, so round out the rest with veggies, protein, and healthy oils. You may even want to add some fiber mix to your diet to clear the track for the climb – just be sure the fiber doesn't kick in too late!

Taper down your activity, and fully rest the day before – not only for rest, but to not deplete your glycogen stores. Your body converts excess glucose into a concentrated form called glycogen. It is stored in your liver and your muscles. A huge problem with carb loading is that your body can become accustomed to this massive intake of carbohydrates. Glycogen gets converted into fat very easily. Only carb load a few times per year to avoid wrecking havoc on your system!

The old method of depleting your stores of glycogen in order to reflexively boost them up to a much higher level has all but been abandoned. This old school method can really mess you up. However, new research has shown that a "quick and dirty" type of carb loading and depletion works very well – possibly boosting your glycogen stores by 90%. This new method suggests that you eat 12grams of carbohydrates (roughly) over a 24 hour period prior to your activity. Before carb loading that day, perform an intensive physical activity such a sprinting (such as doing the aerobic threshold exercise in the cardio section). Then consume your carbs. Eat as much as you can stomach without becoming sick just before you head out, unless you're off at the gates and there would be no time to digest what you just ate.

To help you out further, stay really hydrated the day before and chug plenty of carb and electrolyte loaded water before you go. Chugging water the night before can increase the desire to wake up earlier (an old Native American pre-alarm clock tip).

For high exertion climbs, go heavy on the simple carbs. Figure out how many calories you'll need to eat, and how much water you'll need to drink for the climb or trip. That way when you're packing, you'll at least have an idea of what to go on, even if you can't possibly carry that much food and water.

The point of all these formulas is to basically eat and drink a lot of food and water. If you're aware of how many calories you'll actually spend and how much water you'll need to drink then maybe you'll eat a little better before the climb, pack your meal a bit more intelligently, and have more food in the car. Then maybe you won't bonk as soon and climb a little faster. This could be the thing that gets up you the climb!

VITAMINS AND SUPPLEMENTS
(see injury section for more information on vitamins and supplements)

If you are eating well rounded and balanced healthy meals, you should be fine without needing to add supplements to your diet. But we're always looking for that quick fix or magic bullet. So as far as ergogenic aids are concerned (pills and supplements to make you perform better), do your own research since much of the actual research out there is hit or miss. Exercise and nutrition research is extremely difficult and expensive to conduct, and unfortunately, a lot of research that does get published is quite flawed. Don't believe the hype! I can't stress enough that as long as you eat well and exercise regularly, you will be in great shape and the best way to get better is to just go climbing. Supplements and vitamins for injuries and health conditions have much better research than for exercise performance, so ask your doctor if there's something besides a prescription you can take for what ails you.

Before taking any prescribed or over-the-counter drug or supplement consult with your heath care practitioner to rule out any contraindications or adverse reactions you may experience. Even the most harmless drug can cause an adverse reaction or allergic reaction. Use caution!

VITAMINS
A good multivitamin is the best choice if you're going to take any sort of supplement, so start with the foundation before sailing to the Far East to buy the magic spice. You pay for what you get, so don't get brands like Centrum that are cheap and indigestible. The multivitamin should have far beyond the RDA (recommended daily amount) on most ingredients, and a powder inside a gel capsule is infinitely better then a compressed toilet-clogging hard pill.

138

If you are a male, do not buy a multivitamin with iron unless you have an anemic condition that requires extra iron. Women should get one with added iron because of iron loss through their menstrual cycle. You want one very high in B vitamins (100mg of each would be optimal, or supplement with extra). A standard quality multivitamin usually requires you to take between three to nine gel-caps per day!

To supercharge your multi since they can't fit it all in to a general multivitamin, make your second supplement is a mixture of Calcium, Magnesium, and Zinc (1000g, 600g, 15g per day respectively). The next supplement I would recommend to get is Vitamin D. Some advocate taking 4000 IU per day- so ask your doctor, but 2000IU per day would be a good compromise. Finally, Vitamin C is necessary for recovery and 2000-4000mg a day should suffice for someone highly active.

A supplemental antioxidant isn't a bad idea since you're burning so much fuel. Vitamin E, Selenium, and Alpha-Lipoic Acid are good anti-oxidants. Byproducts of metabolism and outside sources ravage our DNA with "free-radicals". Free radicals are oxygen molecules with ½ an electron desperately looking for something to "oxidize". Anti-oxidants do exactly what the name implies.

Fish-oils and Omega-3 Fatty Acids (4000g per day) are also good to add to your pill-box, or eat oilier fish (check your mercury levels, however). Omega-3 Fatty Acids replace your cell membranes fatty acids, and in doing so, cause you to produce less inflammatory products. These acids help with so many health benefits that increasing the amount you consume can only help…unless you suffer from a few specific conditions (that's why it's a good idea to consult with your doctor when buying a supplement!).

Another good supplement to take on trips is powdered veggie drink mixes. You can find them at health stores. Nanogreens is my favorite, and it claims one packet has some ridiculous amount of servings of fruits and veggies. True or not, it's still a lot easier and lighter than packing vegetables.

Remember to subtract the amount contained in your multivitamin before figuring out how many extra supplemental pills to take.

Recommended for maximum daily health: Multivitamin, B-Complex, Calcium, Magnesium, Zinc, Vitamin D, Vitamin C, Antioxidant Blend, and Fish Oils or Omega-3.

SUPPLEMENTS FOR SPECIFIC CONCERNS
Joint Pain and Arthritis
Glucosamine sulfate (1500mg per day) or Chondroitin sulfate (1200mg per day) are the standard supplements for folks who need to rebuild cartilage in their knees or whatever joint needs repair. Instead of popping ibuprofen or pain killers (they should be called liver, stomach, and kidney killers) go see a chiropractor and a massage therapist regularly.

Pain and Inflammation
Bromelain is a natural anti-inflammatory. Don't take it with food (it's also a digestive enzyme). 4000-5000 MCU per day is a good amount to take with an acute injury. 240g of White Willow Bark is a lot safer for pain and inflammation than aspirin, and will also help with pain and inflammation of an acute injury.

Cold Weather and Circulation
For cold weather try Garlic and Ginko Biloba to help promote blood flow to your fingers and toes. An adult sized tablet of Aspirin taken before a climb can also help thin your blood to help with cold hands and feet. Just make sure you don't have any contraindications with the aspirin.

Sleep
Proven supplements for helping you sleep are Valerian Root and Melatonin. Experiment with the sleeping pills at home! You'd be surprised what messed up dreams can occur with the wrong kind. Over-the-counter sleeping pills are powerful, and should be taken with caution. Some motion sickness tablets and allergy meds contain the exact same ingredients and are a lot cheaper. The two basic "sleeping pill" ingredients are either 25mg of Doxylamine succinate or 25-50 mg of Diphenhydramine hydrochloride. I would seriously avoid taking Ambien in the backcountry since side effects can include severely lucid sleepwalking episodes.

Sickness
When you're sick or getting sick, Echinacea and Zinc lozenges have been shown helpful. There are some fizzy drink mixes that have become extremely popular called "Emergen-C" and "Airborn". It's up to you to decide if those work or not.

Energy and Endurance
For energy and endurance, first change your diet, check for food allergies, and look at your stress levels and sleeping patterns. The following supplements have conflicting reports and results, so make sure all the other bases are covered before possibly wasting your money on the following.

A mega-dose of B-12 in a pill, or by injection is the rage in the celebrity community. Mark Twight recommends Eleuthero and Panax Ginseng. Twight also suggests supplementing with Sodium Phosphate (1 gram every 3-4 hours exercise and 4 grams loading prior to the climb) and Ornathine Alpha-Ketogluterate (2-4 grams three times per 24 hour period during intense exercise – Twin Lab's OKG Fuel is an example of a brand name) to boost endurance and improve recovery. Erik Horst claims that OKG Fuel is a waste of money, and suggests HMB instead (1 gram in morning, 2 grams during activity). Clyde Soles in his climbing manual states that all of the above mentioned energy supplements are garbage. Two recent supplements with a ton of hype, but of course, little research, are Nitric Oxide and Beta-Alanine. Nitric Oxide basically works as a vasodilator, decreasing your "pump". Beta-Alanine is becoming the competitor to Creatine monohydrate (read below).

Finally there are a myriad of energy drinks, coffee (caffeine) and Red Bull being the most popular, although 5-hour Energy brand packs a wallop in a much smaller container. With every up, there's a down – and your body starts to need those drinks to function after awhile. But used carefully, coffee or an energy drink can provide a quick burst of needed energy.

You can spend tons of money and spend countless hours of surfing the internet searching for "research" and opinions on ergogenic aids. I do not recommend any of these supplements.

Strength
The one supplement with the most research is Creatine monohydrate. There are side effects to everything, so read up on it, and use at your own risk. Many athletes have found it useful for high energy explosive movements, but many have reported a diffuse array of negative side-effects that keep them off. As mentioned, Beta-Alanine is becoming a commonly used strength gain supplement. There isn't enough research (but plenty of testimonials!) to say yay or nay to this one, so give it a try and buyer beware. Twin Lab is a reputable source for both of these supplements.

ALTERNATIVES TO SUPPLEMENTS
A great way to get more energy and endurance (if possible) is to live high and train low. Unfortunately you need to either live in Boulder, CO or a city at a high elevation with a substantial drop in elevation to train in – or a lot of cash to buy an artificial sleeping chamber to simulate a higher altitude.

In fact, instead of blowing your paycheck on any of this stuff, try these ideas. Wake up early and go to bed early (like grandpa), sleep for seven instead of eight hours, wake up at the same time every day, eat healthy (cut the sugar, coffee, processed foods and high carb products, red meat, and alcohol – and increase your whole grains, healthy fats, fruits, and vegetables), exercise regularly, have regular sex (sorry single climbers), get a colonic (yikes!), fast occasionally, and engage in mentally stimulating activities. If you're wondering about the 7 hour suggestion, the latest research shows that mortality rates are significantly lower for those who sleep seven versus eight (or less than seven) hours a night!

140

Vantage, WA
Anne Arnoldy Photo

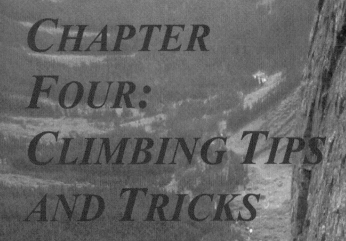

CHAPTER FOUR: CLIMBING TIPS AND TRICKS

Mox Peak, Washington
Eric Wolf Photo

There are a lot of scattered tips throughout this manual, especially in the gear and nutrition sections. This section came about from a slideshow I did in Portland, Oregon.. Watching the audience wide-eyed and slack-jawed in utter shock while listening to some of my advanced alpine climbing "tips", I realized the time had come to put down in writing all the crazy weight saving tricks, rope shenanigans, and gear issues that plague today's modern climber. Instead of writing another "how to" book, this section assumes you already know the basics.

APPROACHING

Bugaboos, Canada
Lane Brown Photo

Sometimes it's fun to blast in and out to your climb car-to-car style, especially if the approach is an uphill grind, or less than four hours. A fit person can hike 2-3 mph on flat trail, and uphill at about 1500 feet per hour regardless of mileage. So, if a section is two miles and 1000 feet, it should still just take about one hour. Intense bushwhacking takes around ½ mile per hour regardless of elevation gain. Your pack weight will ultimately determine how fast your go. A heavy pack (30+ lbs) should only slow you down a bit - because you trained.

When you're hiking in, set a fast pace to start. A slow "all-day" pace is just that, it is slow and takes all day. You don't want to completely waste yourself, but you will most likely be using different muscle groups during the climb. The first hour is always the worst. I usually start hiking as fast as I can until I start to sweat. I then back off just a hair. Hiking out should take 2/3rds the time to hike in, or if it's all downhill, then about ½ the time. You should be wearing just enough to stay warm. In the summer, this usually means just wearing a t-shirt and in all but the coldest conditions, a wind shirt. Overheating and stopping frequently to re-layer adds a lot of time to the day. No matter what type of pack I buy, my hips always wind up getting raw. I tie a rolled-up wind shirt or sweater around my waist to help, and it makes the shirt very handy for stopping or if it gets cold.

Take your breaks before the uphill slog and you'll go faster. Take your breaks either every 1.5 hours, or every 1500-2000 feet. Anymore and you'll tire yourself out from stopping too much. Eat sugar at the breaks with a little bit of fat to carry you through until the next break. Stop for only enough time to eat and fix whatever it is you need to fix, and stop the second you have any discomfort in your feet and fix the problem.

Hide your watch so you're not constantly checking how long you've been hiking and how much altitude you've gained unless you need it for navigation. Have your water handy, preferably in a hydration system like a Camelback. If you know there will be water available on the approach, consider your options. It's lighter to carry less, but it also takes time to fill up, not to mention the loss of momentum and psych you get by stopping all the time. If there will be water about 2 hours into the approach, I will carry 1.5 liters and chug it so I can fill my stomach and the water container at the stream. If the only water is less than 1.5 hours into the approach, I consider stopping to fill a waste of time and energy and will lug the extra water instead of stopping, but it's up to you. If you think the water is safe to drink untreated, carry a wide diameter straw (like from a Slurpee) in your pocket to avoid messing around filling your water containers.

An I-pod will help speed up the hike, but make sure your lonely partner has one too. If you don't have one and your partner does – do not let them tell you what they are listening to! Bring trekking poles if you can stash them at the base of the climb for return pick-up, or if you are camping and can just leave them at camp. If you don't like them, try to get used to them because they make you go faster.

Above: Sometimes it's handy to bring a bike on the trail ... sometimes not
Below: Avoiding the Bushwack   *Justin Thibault Photos*

Red Rocks, NV

If you're sleeping on a long, demanding route you're going to have to sleep cold, hungry, and thirsty to keep the pack weight down enough to climb reasonably well – so what you bring is critical. If you bring a sleeping bag, it shouldn't weigh more than 1-2 lbs…summer or winter. Wear all of your clothes in your bag and make hot water bottles. Ropes and backpacks can be your sleeping pad. If it's really windy, bring the tent fly or a tarp and wrap up in it. You can even share a bag with your climbing partner. Feathered Friends has a two person bivy-bag known as the "Spoonbill". Sleeping pills are helpful. A good bivy kit should only be 1-4 pounds more than your climbing pack without one. A video I-pod and an ear piece per person is a really fun way to kill time at a bivy.

> *Bivy Tip: If you can build a fire, heat rocks in the fire and wrap them in your stove windscreen, freeze-dried food bag, or whatever you can think of to prevent burning yourself. Hot rocks can keep you warm inside your bag for almost the whole night.*

Don't hold your pee. If you didn't bring a piss-bottle, suck it up and go outside or you will never sleep. Have water ready for the morning and your bottles filled before you sleep. If you can spare the gas, a hot water-bottle is a life saver. Just be sure and screw the lid on tight! Eating a high calorie fatty/sugary snack just before you go to sleep will help you keep warm. If you are camping at the base, a good night sleep will drastically increase your chance of success the next day – so bring a nice warm bag, plenty of food and drinks, earplugs, and a alarm that's loud enough to wake you.

If the proverbial poop hits the fan on the climb, start descending if possible. Bivying does nothing but deplete energy and time - unless you really do think the weather, or your partner's injury will get better in the morning. If not, go down. You got up it, you can get down it. Your gear is replaceable. It is a very tough call whether to hunker down or to start descending. Weigh the consequences. Will you be trapped for days in a whiteout or is it just too dangerous to go down? Will your partner's condition worsen or improve? Can he or she even get down? Populated areas are a safer bet since you should eventually reach a road (although many roads are closed in winter). Descending blindly in unpopulated areas could wind up in days of jungle exploration.

It is a very good idea to have a radio to base camp, a personal locator beacon, or at least a cell phone on you unless you truly want to be on your own and live with those consequences. Remember, you put yourself in this predicament and it is up to you, not a rescue team to help you. Not only are you putting others in danger, but helicopters can't fly in bad weather, and not all rescue teams are properly trained and outfitted (depending on where you are). Some rescuers are elite climbers and medics while some are off the couch rednecks who think it's neat to play with ropes and ride in helicopters.

WEATHER AND AVALANCHES

Bendor Range, BC

Learn to read the weather. Sometimes it's not going to rain if it looks grim and sometimes it'll rain on a sunny day. Check the weather like an obsessive compulsive freak days before you go to start seeing patterns. Maybe the bad weather keeps getting pushed back, so if it's cloudy on the hiking day, it may be nice (the opposite can also be true). Don't sleep in when you hear the patter of rain on your tent. If it's raining go anyways – maybe it will be good by the time you are ready to climb. It happens! The website *www.weather.gov* has the most reliable source of weather information.

Keep a journal and write down what you climbed, the date, and reason for failure if applicable. This helps remind you of conditions when you're wondering what to do next year. Talk to locals about the weather patterns, they have a sixth sense that's worth the best meteorologist's six-day forecast. Maybe your range gets thunderstorms at 2pm in August like clockwork, but the forecast doesn't say that. Read the introduction to your guidebooks, they usually have really good tips.

Your altimeter is a handy weather forecast device if you don't have a barometer, or if you haven't been in one spot long enough to get an accurate trend. An altimeter is essentially a barometer configured to give an attitude reading based off the air pressure. If the barometer drops, the altitude will rise, and the risk of bad weather will increase. If you haven't moved in a while and the altitude is 60-80 feet higher, the chance of precipitation is likely – any more than that and a big storm's a brewin' for sure.

Horsetails in the sky and rings around the sun signal storms within 12 to 48 hours. A band of high thin clouds moving in could signal a change from high to low pressure. Lenticular clouds and thunderheads are sure signs that it's time to h⸱⸱ ⸱ down or get off the wall. A great field trick to gauge if a low pressure system or storm is headed tow⸱⸱ ⸱vay from you is to stand with your back to the wind. Wind moves in such a way from high p⸱⸱ ⸱ure that someone figured out that the low pressure system will generally be on your 1⸱ ⸱ facing more westerly, then the storm is moving toward you. If your left side is ⸱ e storm is moving away.

⸱.5 degrees Fahrenheit every 1000 feet, or 2 degrees Celsius every 304 meters, ⸱ this simple freezing level equation. Since temperature inversions are common ⸱tures, this equation can only be used as a good estimate.

Lightning is a huge concern for climbing in high dry areas in the summer months. These storms are often highly predictable and occur almost every day in some locations. Always check the weather and find out when storms usually occur.

There's a phenomenon known as "Group Mentality" where two or more people can convince themselves something to be true, whether or not it's based on any sound judgment. Making up weather forecasts that would encourage bailing or continuing on is a prime example.

Finally, have a Plan B. Plan B's usually never happen because once the bailing mentality kicks in, it's pretty hard to stop it. But if you're ice climbing and there are rocks nearby, bring your rock gear in the car. Bring guidebooks for nearby areas, or places on the way home you can go. Many cancelled ice climbs have resulted in sport-climbing trips with mountaineering boots and double length slings while clad in full Gore-Tex, stinky long underwear, and wet socks.

The basic rule on deciding if avy conditions are too high or not is to decide how badly you want to climb that route that day, because it's ultimately going to come down to that within a certain amount of reason. It's a pain, but carry a beacon at the very least in avy terrain. If you can bring a shovel and probe, that's great! The length and difficulty of the climb and length of the approach will dictate what you're going to bring. Keep up to date on avy forecasts (_www.avalanche.org_), dig pits, listen to the snow pack, keep your eye on the weather and winds, and talk to other climbers.

Most avalanches occur on 35-45 degree slopes, with 38 degrees being the magic number for most dangerous slope angle. You can easily determine the slope angle with a map, or with an inclinometer. If you're on a suspect slope and want to check the angle, try this trick:

Canadian Rockies

Avalanches occur because there is a solid layer of snow over a weak layer of snow. Natural avalanches occur because of new snow from the sky or wind, or a radical change of temperature. Most climbers on steep routes need to be concerned about new snow, temperature changes, wind if they are on the leeward side, and if the climb is threatened from above. On mountaineering routes, approaches, and descents, climbers must be acutely aware of the slope angle and the snow pack's stability.

One quick way to check the snow pack stability is the do a quick test with your ski pole. Feel for hard sliding layers with weak loose layers beneath. At camp or on the approach, isolate a column of snow 1x1 foot wide. Tap on the top with a shovel blade from your wrist, then from your elbow, and finally from your shoulder ten times each – stopping when the snow slides off the column. Poor snow stability would occur if the snow slides from the wrist or if the snow slides off in a planar sheet easily. Fair snow stability occurs if the snow slides from the elbow tap. Good snow stability occurs of the snow only slides from the shoulder taps. A small slope can slide just as easily as a big mountain face, so test the snow on smaller slopes.

Wind will move snow if blowing at 10mph, but most snow is transported at wind speeds 15-80mph, and most of the snow is moved in the 1st couple of hours. The leeward side of the mountain is much more dangerous since this is where all the snow is dumped from the wind.

Mt. Rainier, WA

Shallow snow packs can be much more dangerous than deeper snow packs. One meter of solid snow is generally safe, and over three meters of stable snow should be much safer. The shallower the snow, the more of a temperature difference between the ground, the snow, and the air. Unfortunately this just makes the snow pack get more and more unstable over time. This is why places with a shallower snow packs like Colorado can have high avy danger for months on end. It's important in shallow snow packs to know what the ground is like under the snow. Slabs and heather slide much easier than rough talus fields and treed areas.

Rain severely weakens snow, but a rain crust (or sun crust) ca
falls and bonds to it. If not, a crust acts as the perfect sliding la
snow pack quickly as well.

Follow the mnemonic **ALPTRUTh** to determine if it is safe to go.
then the avy danger is too high.
Avalanches. Have there been recent avalanches in the area in the
Loading. Is there new snow by precipitation, wind, or rain in the la
Path. Will you be in area that is an avalanche path?
Terrain Trap. Couloirs, gullies, trees, and cliffs increase the danger
Rating. Is the current danger rated considerable or worse? Check the
Unstable snow. Are there signs of instability?
Thaw instability. Is there recent warming of the snow pack due to sun, i

NAVIGATION

Check out ***www.fsavalanche.com*** for great videos on avalanche awareness.

FIRST AID AND SELF RESCUE

Jay Hack Photo

Climbing Self Rescue, by Tyson and Loomis, and Medicine for Mountaineering, by James Wilkerson should be required reading (and practice) for every type of climber. The Illustrated Guide to Glacier and Crevasse Rescue, by Tyson & Clelland should be required reading (and practice) for anyone roping up on a glacier. Knowing how to administer basic first aid skills in the mountain environment can save a life. Imagine the guilt you would feel if something happened to your partner and you were helpless to save them because you didn't take the time to bone up on your 1st aid skills.

For those that want to learn more, I highly recommend taking a Wilderness First Responder (WFR) course. NOLS and WMI both provide outstanding courses and refreshers. See *www.nols.edu/wmi* and *www.wildmed.com* for more information. The American Red Cross provides inexpensive CPR and First Aid courses year round at a location nearest you. It is your responsibility not only as a citizen, but to your climbing partner who entrusts their life to you. Check out *www.redcross.org* for more info.

The basic skills you must know are how to maintain an airway, prevent blood loss, perform CPR, and the Heimlich maneuver. I've been in several emergency situations require both self-rescue and 1st aid. I have even managed to choke on a sandwich while bouldering and luckily my partner knew what to do!

The basic skills required for self rescue are: escaping the belay, lowering an injured partner, creating a basic 3:1 or greater hauling system, ascending the rope with prusik-type knots, passing a knot on rappel or while lowering, and evacuating the victim. If you know how to perform these basic skills and tie the more complicated knots (Munter Hitch, Mule Knot, Munter Mule, Garda Hitch, Mariners Knot, Prusik Knot, Autoblock, Klemheist, Bachman, Clove Hitch, Butterfly Knot, Fleishmans Knot) you can come up with a way to get out of all but the most dire situations. These skills are very easy to learn and should only take an afternoon of practice. These skills will leave you if you don't practice them, so try and refresh your skills every six months.

Learn to use a map like you're looking at a picture. Be able to judge how fast you are moving. Read a book on mountain weather, avalanches, and orienteering cover to cover multiple times. Know how to triangulate your position without an altimeter to help you. Don't rely on your partner for getting you there. You need to be able to get there and back just as much as he or she does, so study the guidebook, topo, and maps too.

Take a picture of the topo and map with your digital camera! This does not work well in high glare sunlight, or when your camera dies. Take photos of the route before you climb it to find out where you are on route. Take pictures of the hike out from the summit. It doesn't hurt to bring two topos, two sets of approach and descent info, and two sets of maps. If you have a forced bivy they will make nice fire starters. Topos will smear if kept in your pocket too long. Don't have important information on the crease lines if you're going to fold it.

Google Earth and even better still Microsoft's Virtual Earth software (both are free) are great ways to scope out an approach and descent from home. A GPS is a great tool to have, as is a digital altimeter. Don't trust a digital compass, bring a real one. GPS systems don't always work in bad weather or in the forest, so don't rely on them completely. Consider your GPS as a bonus backup. Set your altimeter at every known point and don't second guess it unless you are at a known point – it's probably more right than you think you are.

If you are hiking off-trail, especially in thick bush, and you get lost, think of the most logical and reasonable solution - not the easiest. In any situation when you are lost, or know you went the wrong way: going all the way back uphill, or retracing your steps even if it's an hour's worth is always much worse sounding than it actually is – and can save your ass. Mountaineering: The Freedom of the Hills should be required reading (and practice) if you don't know how to triangulate your position with a map and compass.

CLIMBING FAST

Before you try and climb every route in record time and in as little pitches as possible, ask yourself, "why do I want to climb this route so fast?" Remember, horsing around with your friends, enjoying a nice lunch halfway up, and talking the time to savor the climbing and scenery could make the climb you planned on blitzing one of the most satisfying memories of your life. That said....

If the difficulty of the climb is at your limit, figure one hour per pitch (leading and following). If it's below your limit then it should take about ½ hour per pitch. To speed it up, do not stop climbing....in other words, just standing there gripping the rock and wondering (because you're probably scared) wastes time. When in doubt, put gear in. When in doubt, put in a belay. Like I said before, just standing there wondering is not climbing fast!

Kong GiGi Set-Up

Don't have a yard sale of gear when you reach the belay if you are cleaning the pitch. With gear that is stuck, you should be thinking to yourself, *"if you got it in, you can get it out"*. At least some amount of blood must be spilt before you can give up. If you can't get it out, it's you're fault, not the leader. Don't waste too much time, however. If you're the follower, rack the gear for the next pitch you're going to lead while you're following. Be ready to lead the moment you get to the belay. You can eat or rest while belaying.

A quick belay change-over uses <u>two</u> belay devices: an auto-locking device such as a Kong Gi-Gi and a regular one such as an ATC. To do this, bring the second up on the auto-block style belay device (which is connected to the anchor or strongest piece) so when the second arrives at the belay, they don't have to tie or daisy in at the belay. While you mess with gear or scan the next pitch, the person who just belayed you up on the autoblocking device can just put you on their regular belay device. When you are ready to go, your partner unclips the autoblock, and viola, you're on a regular lead belay. The extra ounce or two of the added belay device is worth the added time saved at a belay changeover, and also as a back-up if you somehow manage to drop one of them!

If you are leading and you get to the anchor spot, get your gear in ASAP. It is better to have at least one good piece of gear in quickly, than to take forever to make a nice pretty anchor. If you don't have all the pieces you need, the follower will have it on his or her rack and you can beef it up before they lead. If your anchor is sketchy, belay directly off your harness to absorb the follower's weight. If the anchor is solid enough, make an equalized anchor and belay off a power point in your cordelette. If the power point is in an annoying spot, then put the auto-locking device directly on the highest reliable piece. If the second asks if the anchor is good, say *"yes, but don't fall!"*

Yell so loud that you are hoarse by the car to your belayer. If your partner can't hear you, pull all the slack in, put them on belay, and hope they start climbing. If you're the belayer and there is no rope left, yell *"off belay"* regardless, and climb with the speed of the rope pulling up. The follower should not be trying to style the pitch. Pull on gear and commit to holds you might not if you were the leader. You're not going to fall so speed it up!

Always be super mindful of route finding. Pretend like you are the 1st ascensionist. Where would you go? They probably went that way too. Sometimes too specific topo info can mess you up.

Carrying your hiking shoes on the leader's and follower's harnesses separately reduces pack bulk and speeds things up...especially if there's a chimney or off-width section. One pack is generally all that's needed unless it's really cold, or you'll be sleeping on the route. If that's the case, then have one smaller leader's pack, and one heavier followers pack.

A 70 meter rope can speed you up or slow you down. It's heavier and you need to carry 70 meters worth of gear. But if the pitch lengths work out, you can link pitches (assuming you don't run out of gear or have bad rope drag). One 70m can sometimes get you off where you'd need two 60s to rap, thus saving weight and time. You can also chop more rope for rappelling in a pinch. 70's are great for ice climbing or doubled up for simuling.

Simul-climbing can speed things up vastly. If you're the leader and you had a hard time with a section, put a belay in just before the follower gets to that point. You can climb a hard pitch with the second following easier terrain, but not the opposite. You need lots of gear to simul climb, so put it in at strategic locations. Clipping a Tiblock (worse for the rope) or Ropeman (better for the rope) to a piece of gear can make simul-climbing safer. If the follower falls, all their weight will come onto the piece of gear with the mini-ascender on it. The downside is this creates a lot of rope drag. You may need to double your rope to decrease rope drag. If climbing with a lead line and a rappel line, put the rappel line in the pack instead of dragging it up the route.

Climbing in a team of three can be a great way to save weight by spreading out group gear three ways instead of two. You can even bring some extra gear (and food/gas). The leader leads up, and belays the next climber. When that climber reaches the belay, he or she should immediately start belaying the leader and the 3rd at the same time. After a few pitches, the leader can swap positions with the other two in the crew. On easier terrain the team of three can have the two followers climb simultaneously. The leader can either belay the team on two ropes at the same time with the followers slightly staggered, or the leader can belay both on the same rope. To belay both on the same rope, the first follower ties in with a Butterfly knot about 20 feet above the end of the rope, and the 3rd ties in at the end. If the 3rd falls, the purpose of the butterfly knot is to keep the pull of the rope in line and off of the 2nd.

"Short Fixing" is another way to speed up the climb. This is most commonly used in aid climbs where the leader doesn't have to belay the 2nd up because they are jugging the line. While the second jugs, the leader begins leading the next pitch using clove hitches, a Gri-Gri, or a self-belay device. When the second reaches the anchor, he or she then puts the leader on belay. This situation could be used in free-climbing if the second jugs instead of follows, but probably won't be much faster unless both climbers are dialed at jugging fast and rope-soloing quickly. But if the pitch the 2nd is jugging is very difficult and the grade of next pitch is fairly tame, this tactic could really speed things up although not as much fun for the follower since he or she is jugging instead of climbing.

Leading in blocks can keep the team focused, and focus and intent is what really speeds up a climb. It is probably faster to tie into the rope with two locking carabineers and a figure-8 on a bight, but if you didn't bring a bunch of lockers, then just tie in regular-style. The point is to have the same leader for a bunch of pitches in a row. After a few warm-up pitches, the leader and follower get into their positions and really start to haul-ass. Switch it up after the leader starts to get tired, or spooked. I think the stronger leader should go first to set the pace, even though he or she won't be as tired for the 2nd block to be led.

Illumination Rock, OR

AID AND FRENCH FREE

For short sections of aid, you can fashion etriers out of your cordelette by tying a small figure-8 on a bight in the middle, and two small figure-8s on a bight at the tail ends. Pull a bight of cord through the tails and girth hitch your feet by slipping your feet inside the loop. Use your daisy and either a double length sling or two should length slings girth hitched together to clip into gear. There are also lightweight alpine aiders available if the climb requires enough aid to warrant bringing these.

Etriers fashioned from a Cordelette

Trucks are aid. Radek Chalupa Photo.

To jug the line, I highly recommend packing the extra weight of two ascenders to speed things up. Tiblocks and Ropemen will shred the rope and take forever to clip and re-clip comparatively – however, if you weren't expecting to jug, then you'll be glad you brought these instead of prusiking up the rope!

Hooking, piton placement, stacking gear, cam hooking, and copperheading can all be used for short aid sections on an otherwise free route. They turn a horrifying run-out into something slightly more do-able during free climbing. Practice these gear placement skills on some chossy rock so you can become more confident in the mountains.

French Freeing is way faster than busting out the aid gear, so if you have (and can spare) the energy, try pulling your way through each placement. Step on gear, call "take" at each piece, and step in slings. If you're partner doesn't have ascenders for the French Free section, be sure to clip long slings to the hard sections so he or she can also yard through.

For an extremely detailed lesson in aid and big wall technique, Chongo has written the bible. It is for sale online at *www.chongonation.com* for a hefty $125 as of press time. Chris McNamara over at *www.supertopo.com* is writing a new book on Aid and Big Wall technique and should be available soon.

RAPPELLING

Mt. Triumph, Washington

Backing up the Rappel

Who said rappelling isn't fun?! After reading this section, you may be giddy with joy when it comes time to descend.

Cleaning gear on rappel on an overhanging sport climb is always difficult. Clip a quickdraw into your belay loop and to the line that's not going through the gear to stay in line with the climb. If all the weight of the rope is pulling against a quickdraw, making it difficult to unclip, clip your belay loop quickdraw directly into the quickdraw you are trying to remove. This puts your weight on the draw, not the rope, so you can now unclip the rope and remove the draw. Always keep a bail biner on your harness so you don't have to leave a draw if you can't make it up the climb.

Use an overhand knot to connect the ropes if they are a similar diameter (aka the Euro Death Knot). Two overhands snugged up against one another should suffice if the ropes are slightly different sizes. Use a Fleishman's knot if they are very different sizes. This is like a water knot used to tie runners together, except with a figure-8 instead of an overhand. Have the 1st rappeller do a test pull to make sure the rope won't get stuck. Back up the rappel for the 1st rappeller with a piece of gear and a long enough sling clipped to the rope so that the sling is slack.

The heaviest partner always goes first with a back-up that the 2nd will remove. If the ropes are of equal size, you and your partner weight the same with packs on, the anchor is bomber, and the next anchor is visible with no rope issues, simul-rappel. It's way faster and not very difficult. If your partner is much heavier than you, then wear the heavier pack. Just make sure to weight and un-weight the rope at exactly the same time.

When rappelling with a 6mm tag line make sure you don't die if the 6mm rope gets the chop while rappelling. To do this, try the following set-up. This set-up requires you to pull the 6mm first because it has a much greater chance of snarling on something when it comes tumbling down. The con to pulling the 6mm first is that if the rope gets really stuck early on during the pull, you have to jug or lead back up on the 6mm rope! Careful attention to detail will decrease your chances of a stuck rope. Are there rope eating cracks? Are there lips that will hang up the knot? Are there bushes, rock horns, or chicken heads that will catch and loop around the rope?

Rappel set up for pulling a 6mm rope:
1. Put the knot so the skinny rope is on the end you pull, and <u>under</u> the anchor
2. Since there will be rope slippage, make sure that the knot won't sneak its way into the anchor and get jammed. Two ways to do this are keep the knot several feet below the anchor (impossible in a hanging situation). Or, tape the anchor hole smaller so there is only room for the rope to slide through.
3. Just above the rope connection knot (a Fleishman's knot works well ...i.e. a re-woven fig-8), but below the anchor, tie an overhand on a bight in the fat rope.
4. Clip a fat, rounded locking biner (less chance of it getting caught) into the overhand on a bight, and clip that around the skinny rope. It's hard to visualize, but if the skinny rope gets the chop while your rapping down, you'll now be fully on the fat rope as if doing a fixed single rope rappel since the overhand with the biner will be cinched around the anchor.
5. You must pull the skinny rope in this situation. Do a test pull to make sure you set it up correctly.

Rope to pull fed UNDER the anchor. Tape added to keep knot from sliding through the anchor.

Overhand knot tied on lead rope on the side that will be pulled, clipped to itself on the side that won't be pulled. If the skinny rope breaks, this is what keeps the systems still attached to the anchor.

A 6mm rap line tied with a Fleishman's (fig-8 follow through) to the lead line. This is the strand to pull.

Pull

One way to ensure the skinny rope doesn't snarl up when tossing it down is to stuff the rope into a small lightweight stuff sack with the end tied to the drawstring. Toss the stuff sack and the rope will feed really well. The problem with this is not only can the bag get caught and be impossible to free (not good at all), but it is incredibly annoying and time consuming to stuff 60meters of thin cord into a small stuff sack.

To avoid rope snarls when tossing the lead rope, coil the rope into two stacks. Toss the non-free end stack first and then toss the free end stack last. A bit more tedious, but completely snarl free way to rappel is to have each rope lap coiled in separate stacks which are secured by a doubled-up shoulder length slings, feeding out the rope as you rappel.

Tyler Adams Photo

For unknown rappels, put your rappel device in the second loop closest to your harness on your daisy chain. Tie an autoblock knot with your perlon that you had on your harness (see gear section) below the rappel device and clip the loop to your leg loop. Be aware where the ends of the rope are! Knots in the end are good, but sometimes they get caught and you can't pull the rope up or down which is probably the worst situation ever! Never tie both ropes together at the bottom.

Belay Device Attached to First or Second Loop in Daisy Chain

Autoblock Knot Below Belay Device and Above Brake Hand

Autoblock Knot Clipped into Leg Loop of Harness

Autoblock Back-Up Rappel Set-Up

156

Picket Range, WA

If the rope is stuck from below and you can't pull up enough rope to rap down and free it, you'll have to down prusik the rope (be sure to fix the end to the anchor!). If the rope is really stuck in an area you can't free it (like in a wide crack), you have no choice but to chop your rope. If you're feeling randy, tie a figure-8 on a bight on the tail of the chopped rope, put a back-up piece of gear in, and rap from the stuck rope! This is for emergency use only, so ONLY do this if your life depends on the extra amount of rope gained from this little stunt.

If the rope is stuck from above and won't pull, first try walking back away from the cliff as far as possible (and if possible). If that doesn't work, try flipping the rope a bunch. That didn't work? Maybe you're pulling on the wrong end. No? Well now try this: pull hard very quickly and let go very quickly a few times to rubber band the jammed section out of whatever it's stuck in. Still stuck? Now is the time to pull really really hard. Put yourself back on rappel and use your body weight to help you and your partner pull. Look out for falling debris if the rope comes unstuck! I have pulled too hard and snapped the ropes, so be careful here.

Wait, it's still stuck? Dear god! Now you have to try leading up on whatever rope you have pulled down. If there's not enough rope for that and <u>both</u> lines are within reasonable reach, you can prusik, jug, or use your belay device to "Batman" up both ropes to free the knot since it's obviously still through the anchor. Your partner can put you on a fireman's belay if you are yarding yourself up with your belay device. The latter is probably the quickest way to get back up there if the terrain is difficult but not overhanging. If at least one rope is down, use it to lead back up to the anchor.

Let's say you've pulled the other end of the rope way out of reach and now it's stuck, or the rope got stuck on something tumbling down and none of these tricks have worked. You are about to embark on one of the most miserable experiences of your life. The procedure described below is essentially rope-soloing with the added bonus of your stuck rope for security above. Yeah, right! I'm sure you'll be psyched on that if you get stuck in this situation!

Have your partner belay you on the stuck line, or if they aren't in the picture, tie the end of the stuck rope to the anchor with enough slack to tie clove hitches in or figure-8's on a bight on the way up (two feet of slack should be good). You are now going to have to climb the rock and slide the clove hitch up (or tie in with fig-8's constantly) while putting in tons of gear. Tie a clove hitch on the stuck rope to your harness on a locker or two, and start climbing back up, sliding the clove hitch up as you go. If you're paranoid, you can tie two separate

157

clove hitches. If it's too steep to deal with the clove hitch, tie and re-tie multiple figure-8 on a bight backup knots, and climb on the limited amount of slack you gave yourself tied to the anchor.

If the is no way to re-climb, or at least to aid back up, you have a choice to make. Either cut the rope and use what you have to complete the descent, or prusik up the rope which could be stuck on virtually nothing. Your rappels will be shorter and you'll probably lose a lot of gear to make quasi-safe anchors. Scrounge around your stuff to see what you can rappel off of safely. Jammed knots, home-made chockstones from loose rocks and gravel, webbing from your backpack, hell you can rap off anything as long as it's jammed in solid enough! If you must have all of your rope to rappel because the way down is an overhanging crack-less nightmare, you may have to jug your stuck line on prusiks. I've seen ropes stuck that will hold two climbers body weight trying to free it that's literally just holding onto a micro ledge and the side of the tape at the end of the rope. Prepare to vomit during this unique little experience. With this in mind, never have any tape on the rope, so cut it off the ends before you leave home.

Temple Crag, CA

If you think the rope might get stuck in the anchor, have the first rappeller do a test-pull. Be sure to communicate this, as the 2nd may freak out if he or she starts seeing the rope slide through the anchor! If it looks like the rope will get stuck, the 2nd can slide the knot as far away from the anchor as possible (make sure the rap isn't a rope-stretcher because you may not have enough rope to make it to the anchor). If the 2nd can't slide the knot down, then while on rappel, brake the rope you're going to pull and feed out the other rope – effectively sliding the knot down as you rap. This can be difficult because of friction – but is possible. Also, make sure the two ropes aren't twisted. Check the anchor before you head down, and put your leg between both strands to de-tangle any twists.

When rapping off ice routes: do not forget the simple elegance and strength of a well made bollard. Instead of threading webbing or sling material through a V-thread hole, just thread the rope through the screw hole itself. Have the first rappeller do a test pull to make sure it will pull and the rope didn't freeze inside the hole. When the 2nd rappeller gets to the new anchor, pull the rope ASAP to avoid it freezing in place. V-threads are common-place for rappelling. However, recent studies have shown that vertically oriented V-threads are stronger than horizontally oriented ones – and just as easy to make.

Sport climbers lowering off overhanging routes can ease the cleaning of draws by clipping in directly to the quickdraw from a free quickdraw clipped to their belay loop. This takes the pull of the rope off the draw it's going through. After you've clipped to the draw, unclip the rope. Now pull in quick and unclip both draws from the bolt. Don't forget to clip your free draw (attached to your belay loop) to the rope going up to the anchors to stay in-line and close to the wall.

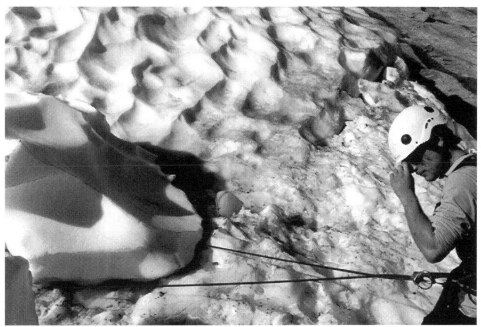

Not the safest bollard   *Justin Thibault Photo*

Standing Rock, Utah

Retrievable single rope rappel trick: *Here's a MacGyver-esque rappel trick that involves a Fifi Hook and a Rubber Band. It allows you to do a full rope rappel off of one rope with the ability to retrieve the rope. The Fifi Hook will need a hole at the top, and you can drill one of yours doesn't have one. The rubber band should be sturdy since the recoil is what gets you your rope back.* **TRY THIS SET-UP IN A CONTROLLED TEST FIRST, AND IN DIRE SITUATIONS ONLY!** *Attach the end of the rope to the Fifi Hook, leaving some tail. Girth hitch the rubber band around the Fifi Hook and loop it under the tail so that the band is tight enough to pull the daisy out of the rappel sling (see photo). The scary part isn't weighting the rope, but in releasing weight from the rope. Even though the rope requires some tugs to spring the hook free, it is a safe bet not to un-weight the rope during rappel, until you are on the ground or secured to an anchor. The hook can definitely get caught up on the way down, or hit and injure you. However, the light weight of a Fifi Hook and a rubber band may be worth it if you ever really need to use this insane looking rappel set-up.*

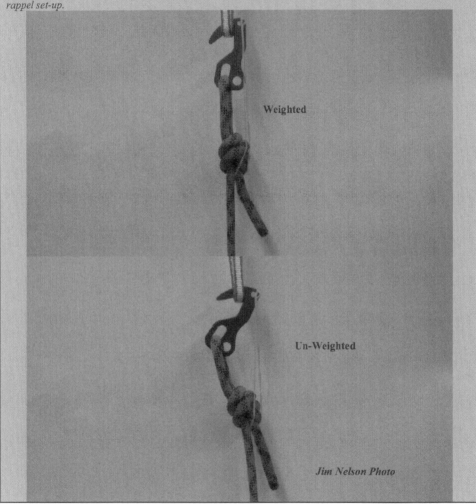

Weighted

Un-Weighted

Jim Nelson Photo

Freeing a stuck rope (looped over a rock horn). In this illustration there was not enough free rope to re-lead. Instead of prusiking off the stuck rope, the leader is rope-soloing with a clove-hitch while placing gear. If the wall was unclimbable, the leader would have to prusik the rope. The belayer has the rope locked off and is providing just enough slack for the leader to slide the clove hitch up the line and to provide a dynamic belay. The rope could be tied off to the anchor if the leader was alone.

BOLTING AND ANCHOR PLACEMENT:

BY JAMES GARRETT W AND MICHAEL LAYTON

Almost all climbers clip bolts or use chain anchors that someone else installed. The people that put up these climbs and install these anchors are climbers just like you and me. This section is for the good Samaritan who sees a ratty anchor and wants to replace it. There is no government agency that keeps climbs up to date, so it is up to us. I (M.L.) have also included a basic "how to" on drilling and placing bolts for those of you who want to put up some climbs that require bolts. Don't expect that "someone" else to do it for you. "Someone" went through all the trouble to make all these climbs for you, the least you can do is help keep them nice!

Of course this brings in the ethical debate. Bolts are here and have been for a long time. Even our "hardman" forefathers placed bolts back in the day. There are some ground rules, however. As the first ascensionist, you get to determine where to place the route, and the bolts. Make sure that the route isn't contrived and squeezed in. Follow the style of the crag, lest you be shunned from that local climbing community. Don't add bolts to an established route without either the consent of the FA team, or a general consensus of the climbing community – the same goes with chopping bolts.

It is best to protect the climb for a lead of that grade. A 5.8 climb should be protected for a leader who climbs 5.8/5.9's…etc. However, over-bolted routes can take away from some scary fun. On the flip side, what's the point of making a route run-out if you're just creating a sport climb? Also, if you are 6 feet 7 inches tall, be considerate of others shorter than you leading the route. Bolted climbs are put up for posterity, so make them quality routes. Not everything needs a line on it. You will get criticism no matter what you do. Just don't bolt next to a crack unless the crag is purely sport and the crack is very short and insignificant.

Think of the future when you put up a bolted line. It may become extremely popular. If no trail existed before, you can bet that a trail will exist after a few parties climb it. Do you want the blank mountain face in the pristine wilderness to have a ride up it? Just because you can't climb it and need a bolt ladder doesn't mean someone else won't be able to later. Bolts can make an area great, or ruin an area. Stupid short crags on the highway side may be okay for grid bolting, but maybe not so in a well established area with classic problems.

Unfortunately, many of the bolts being placed today may in fact be unsafely or incorrectly installed. Most often, when a subsequent climber is repeating a bolt protected climb or rappelling from bolted anchors, the climber has little idea what lies below the surface of the bolt he is using. The climber inherently trusts the people who have placed those bolts before him. When it comes to bolts and hangers, looks are everything.

> *An example in the other direction was driven home to me when I (J.G.) once placed a two bolt belay/rappel anchor atop a two pitch climb in Ibex quartzite (renowned for its hardness). I had placed two 3/8" x 3" bolts. One was a Hilti Stud and the other was a Powers (5 piece blue band Rawl). 3/8" chain was quick-linked to both hangers, however, one hanger was a modern Metolius hanger and the other was a thin, but intact Leeper hanger (the standard for the 60's - 80's). the route is unquestionably 3-star, however, the only comment I received from a well known climber who does frequent bolting forays in the Wasatch was that it was "dangerous" anchor....it was not a safe rappel. He only knew what he could see, and it didn't look good to him...at other times, it may look good, but could be rusted out or fractured below.*

When I (J.G.) hear from first ascensionists who claim to just do such climbs "for themselves" yet report the climbs in the press and guidebooks, I am often led to wonder how much responsibility they actually feel for the climbers who will follow them on these new routes. For me, it would be a horrific lifelong burden to carry if another climber was killed or seriously injured due to an anchor failing that I had placed. I try to be as responsible to the craft as I possibly can.

Style (how you are drilling the climb be it on lead or on rappel) and also the kind of climb you are establishing will dictate choice of equipment to some extent, however, most areas consider the old Rawl drive ¼" button head bolts to be an inappropriate size.

That said, what follows is some basic instructions on how to bolt and put in anchors.

EQUIPMENT

Like a professional carpenter or tradesman, a first ascensionist who will be placing bolts or equipping a route should use the proper tools. Quality is a variable here that should not be ignored. Furthermore, the right tool for the job should always be your maxim. Disdain from half measures. Economics should neither have a role in the quality of the bolts/equipment used nor in the quantity placed on the route. There is no substitute for safety, and safety is why we are drilling the bolts in the first place.

First let us discuss making the hole. Drilling by hand with a hand drill is cheaper and more appropriate for remote areas or for an "emergency" bolt kit. Drilling a "perfect" and symmetrical hole for the bolt is more difficult than with a battery powered industrial grade drill. Drilling by hand is also somewhat of a lost craft for it requires experienced skill to achieve a quality result. Inevitably, if drilling many new routes, a power drill may be chosen to accomplish this task for most cases. When shopping, choose a tried and proven model that offers battery power longevity, light weight, and has a chuck size for SDS type rock drill bits that have become the standard. These are available in 6" lengths and hence, usually can drill a hole to accommodate most bolt length sizes. You will need a bolt hammer or wall hammer, a wrench to fit the bolt, a bulb or tube to clean the hole (and a brush if necessary), and chalk-bag or similar carrying device to keep your bolts, hangers, and bits in.

Hand Drills

A variety of manufacturers produce these hand drills both for the climbing and industrial world. The type of holder will usually dictate the types of drill bits you use. Popular in the last 10-15 years is the wilderness hand drill that accommodates standard SDS bits more commonly used with the Hilti, Bosch, Milwaukee, or Ryobi power hammer drills. Whichever one you choose or end up with, familiarize yourself with its operation and practice on some piece of rock or concrete around the house before you really need it up on some wall.

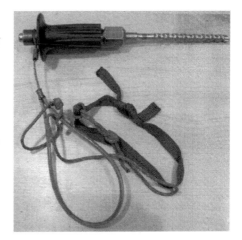

A couple of usage tips for hand drills:
- *Make sure the bit is firmly attached and secure in the holder.*
- *Use sharp drill bits for maximum efficiency.*
- *Put athletic tape on the bit to the desired hole depth*
- *Hold the hand drill quite loose in your hand and perpendicular to the rock. Observe almost a jackhammer effect during the hammer strikes*
- *Frequent light taps seem more effective than major pounding with the hammer.*
- *Moreover, very hard strikes with the hammer and holding the hand drill too tightly in your hand will lead to bit breakage.*
- *Use protective eye wear.*
- *As you tap/drill rotate the holder/drill bit in the direction of the spirals of the bit...usually clockwise.*
- *Be patient, get into a rhythm, try to drill as uniform hole as possible.*
- *Tap, rotate, clear dust, and drill deep enough.*

Power Drills

If you are buying a power drill, you have probably decided to go for it and get serious about drilling bolts. Remember, it is an expensive and thankless job. Furthermore, no matter how well you learn to do it and maybe even manage to fashion quality climbing routes from blank faces; no matter how much you perfect the craft, how well you protect that 5.8 bolted slab for the fledgling 5.8 leader, most the feedback you hear will be critical.

With that said do some research and even go to the outlets and try the tools out before you dish out the kind of cash necessary to purchase one. Ryobi makes a gas powered

drill which doesn't require a bunch of battery packs, so it can drill more holes if you aren't able to recharge. Test your drill out on a practice rock at home to see how many holes your drill will make. The softer the rock, the more holes you can drill so take that into account, especially when drilling on hard rock. On road trips you can buy an A/C inverter to recharge the batteries in your car.

SDS Bit with Tape for depth guidance

Hold the drill with the drill bit as perpendicular (90 degrees) to the rock as possible. Start drilling holding the drill firmly in place; yet loose enough to allow the "hammer jack" effect for maximum efficiency. In hard rock, it can spare your bits to either change bits mid hole or move it in and out drilling the hole in stages. Drill bits are an additional expense, and dull ones do you two specific disservices. Dull bits can drill too narrow of a hole for the bolt you intend to insert, and dull bits drain your battery power rapidly.

Find a solid section of rock with a flat surface and go through your mental checklist:
- *Take some time to tap with your hammer and avoid hollow, uneven, or loose sections of rock.*
- *Once you have decided that you have found a good place to drill, double check to see if this is also a natural place to clip the bolt for the lead climber.*
- *Can you easily drill a perpendicular hole and install a bolt/hanger which will not be impeded by surrounding rock?*
- *Will the carabineer or quick draw hang freely unimpeded by rock edges (that could break any carabineer in a fall?*
- *Do I have the proper size and type of bolt and drill bit for the type of rock I am drilling in?*
- *Am I familiar with the hammer drill or hand drill? And can I properly use the tool I have chosen?*
- *Do I have all the other tools I may need to finish the job?*
- *Always hesitate before you drill and ask yourself the additional questions:*
- *Do I really need a bolt here?*
- *Shall I really make this permanent change to the rock?*
- *Am I prepared? Will I do a good job?*
- *Do I have the proper tools?*

"A clean hole is a healthy hole"! a master once taught me (J.G.). After drilling a little deeper than you may actually need, vigorously blow or scrub the dust out of the drilled hole. In sandstone especially, a dirty or improperly prepared hole often leads to what is called a "spinner", a bolt that does not seat well, does not tighten properly, and is left with a loose hanger that "spins" around. When encountered on a route, these are hardly confidence inspiring for the lead climber. Occasionally, they are indeed time bombs.

Avoiding the spinner
- *Use an extended plastic tubing or micro bulb hose to adequately blow out and extricate the drill dust.*
- *A steel or fiber industrial hole brush can also be very efficient. This is key for installing glue-in bolts which require a super clean hole for the best result.*
- *In soft rock, be sure to use a sleeved multi-piece expansion bolt and very slightly expand it prior to tapping it into the hole.*
- *Drill a hole deep enough and wide enough for the particular bolt to be placed. Correct hole preparation usually prevents a spinner.*
- *Remove any tape such as is often found on the popular Powers (formerly Rawl) 5 piece sleeve expansion bolts.*
- *Avoid using dull drill bits which may create too narrow of a hole and in turn cause the bolt to buckle or bend when trying to force into the hole.*

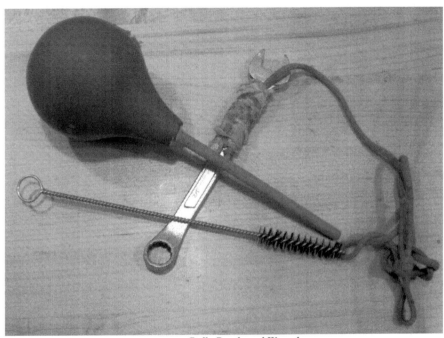

Bulb, Brush, and Wrench

The Right Bolt for the Job
Selecting the proper bolt for the hole should not be under emphasized. Many types of rock exist and require different types of methods, but essentially we will refer here to "hard" rock (quartzite, granite, basalt, and some limestone and some conglomerate) and "soft" rock (sandstone, some limestone, and some conglomerate). This is often subjective and one may be certainly drilling in other rock types not mentioned above. Ultimately, the driller must be responsible here and assess whether the rock is in the hard or soft category, for each requires different equipment. Almost all bolts which work well in soft rock may function equally well in hard rock if correctly placed, however, inversely; this is not the case at all.

Sleeve and stud type expansion bolts may be purchased in a variety of locations, from Home Depot and Hilti Outlets to climbing shops. The hangers needed for them can only be found in climbing shops or via the internet sites available such as for Fixe, Petzl, Metolius, and others.

Left to Right: Hanger, 2 wedge style bolts, 2 expansion sleeve style bolts, machine bolt, buttonhead and rivet hanger, pin bolt, dowel bolt, and 2 glue in bolts (bottom).

Glue-In Bolts versus Expansion Bolts

A Swiss Mountain Guide friend of mine (J.G.) who has done extensive bolt testing and bolt placement in Switzerland once shared his preference for glue-in bolts in this way: A glue-in bolt is only under stress, once placed, when it is weighted or fallen on or otherwise stressed by a climber. On the other hand, an expansion bolt, by its very nature is always under stress for its entire life. It then makes sense to assume that the glue-in variety would get all the gold stars for longevity, strength, weather resistance (they are almost always manufactured from stainless steel or titanium), durability, and function. With that said, why aren't they used more often in the United States?

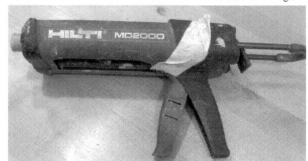

Glue Gun

166

Soft Rock Bolts

Due to the numerous pieces consisting of a sleeve style expansion bolt, these are usually a bit more expensive than a "stud" or wedge bolt. Some type of cone is at the tip and as it is tightened, the sleeve expands over the entire depth of the hole. This is why it is usually far superior to an angle piton being pounded into a smaller sandstone hole. Arguments for drilled angles are many, but the main problem that exists for them is that more than 90% of the time they are just simply placed improperly.

Minimal size used should be 3/8" (12mm) x 3". Remove any tape securing the cone to the bolt and sleeve prior to placement. This could prevent the bolt from expanding properly. I (J.G.) have also found that applying a little weight such as clipping a quickdraw to the hanger after I have tapped the sleeve bolt and hanger flush with the rock while tightening, can be fruitful for preventing spinners. You want to tighten the bolt more than finger tight, but not so tight you break the head off the bolt.

Theory Behind Drilled Angles

If the rock is too soft for a sleeve type expansion bolt (it won't expand enough after tightening and results in a spinner), then why not pound a ½" angle piton into a 3/8" hole? Angle pitons taper in width throughout its length. Unless the installer drills with two to three different bit sizes the length of the same hole, one can visualize that very little of the piton will actually be making expansive contact with the sides of the hole. A few perfectionists such as Olevsky in Utah's Zion Navajo Sandstone will actually painstakingly do this and the bolts are bomber. He will often also insert epoxy into the hole prior to pounding the piton into the rock as well. This is rarely done this meticulously, however, and therefore most drilled angles on sandstone routes should be viewed with suspicion.

Hard Rock Bolts

In the marble like hard quartzite of places like Ibex, Utah, stud type bolts, even as short as 3/8" x 2 ¼" can be excellent and long lasting protection. These wide cone type wedge bolt plugs on the tip of a threaded bolt can be simply pounded into the drilled hole. Put the hanger, washer, and nut onto the stud down the shaft at least a 1/8" while pounding it in. If your hammer blows miss the mark and damages the threads during this process, if the nut is already on, you may be able to salvage the placement.

Few climbers like to approach a bolt and see the stud sticking out more than 1/16" above the nut. Screw the nut back flush before the final blows of the hammer. Then tighten the nut. The threads ideally will just barely be peeking out from above the top of the nut. You want to tighten the bolt more than finger tight, but not so tight you break the head off the bolt.

Drilling the hole deeper than needed is always a good idea. You are guaranteed to avoid the "looking at an inch of thread" syndrome and also if you did damage the bolt and need to remove it or replace it, it can be countersunk after chiseling off the top and patched. Viola, the bolt or scar or "chop" job disappears. With sleeve bolts, these can be much easier removed and new or SS bolts can take their place.

It's a good idea to shop around before you buy a bunch of bolts. You'll want to know what type of rock (hard or soft), the climate (wet or dry), and the type of route (alpine or sport) you'll be doing. Here are some good places to get a good idea on what's out there when buying bolting and anchor equipment before you start shopping at the local hardware store.

- **Fish Products**: _www.fishproducts.com_
- **Pika Mountaineering**: _www.pikamtn.com_
- **Fixe**: _www.fixeusa.com_
- **Petzl**: _www.petzl.com_
- **Metolius**: _www.metoliusclimbing.com_
- **MEC**: _www.mec.ca_
- **Mountain Gear**: _www.mountaingear.com_

Climate Considerations

Getting the longevity and extended life from a bolt placement has more to with learning what it has working against it than perhaps for it. Again, responsibility, judgment, research, and intelligence come into play here.

If the bolt will be frequently exposed to wet or snowy conditions, stainless steel, despite its expense, should be strongly recommended. It has been found in sea cliff areas even a stainless steel bolt with a SS hanger corroded at very rapid rates. "Mixing the metals" was often the blame. Hence, in many such areas such as Cayman Brac and Thailand, the use of stainless steel or better yet, titanium glue-ins are the only things that seem to last longer than a few years!

BOLTING ON LEAD AND RAPPEL

When bolting on rappel, use a Gri-Gri with a prusik-type back-up knot. It's a good idea to top-rope the route and tick the bolt locations with chalk to ensure a good location for bolt placement. Nothing makes a route more annoying (or dangerous) than poor spacing between bolts, hard to clip stances, having the rope run in a dangerous location behind your leg, or having your biners lay over edges after you've clipped a bolt.

When bolting on lead, keep in mind that other may not be as brave as you. You may need to hang off gear, or if you can, find no hands stances. It's handy to carry a few hook, nuts, cams, and even pitons. Just as long as what you are hanging off of will hold you body weight. Many bolts have been placed on lead while hanging off of one arm, or on A4 placements! Make sure you have your drill and all of your equipment tied off to a shoulder sling or your harness.

One trick **to avoid climbing with the weight of the drill** is to leave it hanging off your last bolt on a fifi hook attached to a haul line. Have the haul line come up from the drill to a biner clipped to your harness, and back down to the belayer. As you climb up, the slack goes through the biner. When you need to haul, just pull up the haul line. Your belay can even pull down on the haul line going through your biner to bring the drill up to you, but this can pull you off the wall if you are not careful!

An idea for **bolting sections that require closely spaced bolts** is to drill two bolts on each end of a 2x4 piece of wood connected by a piece of cord. Clip the 2x4 into the bolt you just drilled as a platform to stand on to drill the next bolt.

EMERGENCY BOLTING IN THE ALPINE OR BIG WALL

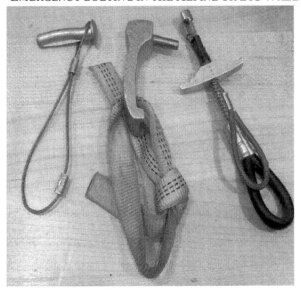

Some alpine or big wall routes require bolts to make it through blank sections of rock. If you are climbing a close to the road soon to be classic, please take the time to place solid bolts. But if you need "emergency" bolts, there are some options. You'll need a hand drill and one or two sharp bits. You can place removable bolts in the holes if you are lucky enough to own a few. An option used mostly for aid is to place the bolt without a hanger and using a rivet hanger over the bolt end. If you need that bolt for free climbing to save your butt in case of a serious fall, but still don't want to carry heavy 3/8" expansion bolts, you are excused and may use ¼" or even buttonhead bolts. Just remember, your route may become a classic – and remember how much fun it is to clip sketchy buttonhead or stardrives on old school routes?

Left to Right: Buttonhead and homemade rivet hanger, bolt-hole hook, removable bolt camming device

BELAY STATIONS AND ANCHORS

Using hefty bolts is always the "rule" for belay and rappel stations. There are no excuses for installing poor bolted stations. Bolts installed should be longer and fatter than perhaps the bolts protecting the route if applicable.

Much has been written about anchor equalization. This is certainly true with less than bomber quality ¼" bolted or trad belays. Aged sling and webbing is just not as strong as chained anchors. Many manufactured chain type rappel and belay anchors no longer utilize equalization theories to counteract the deathly potential of "shock loading" an anchor.

As long as at least 3/8-5/16" proof-grade or high-grade chain is quick-linked (2 links per chain is better than one) tightly with a wrench to at least two beefy bolts in good rock, and the rappel is taken from a point, rarely do problems arise. Other anchor setups can use bolts with rappel rings, or Metolius rap bolts, or for short sport route a pair of cold shuts. The configuration can vary as frequently as the first ascensionists, yet still be very safe.

Of course, the standard bomber side by side (separated by at least 6") bolts with two pieces of chain is also very recommended. With the odd number of links into a quick-link attachment to the hanger, you are guaranteed to find the rope threading a link that is sitting 90 degrees from the wall, instead of flat against the wall, and easy rope retrieval.

Stacked washer setups through the chain avoiding the use of a hanger is old school, but no longer acceptable. When encountering them, you never seem to know how much of that bolt is actually in the rock! Don't be a cheapskate when setting up permanent anchors.

Regular sport climbers are in the habit of lowering off of their own locking carabineers or quick draws if the route is going to be climbed or top roped by another climber in their group. But when an experienced climbers accompanies beginners to the crag, they may be reluctant to leave them with the task of untying at the anchors, rethreading through the chains, and otherwise cleaning the route. For safety reasons, this is understandable. Under these conditions on a high traffic route however, these chains may begin to show wear very quickly. This very scenario is the chief reason it is so important to use heavy steel chain links or buck up and pay for stainless steel rap rings to be added. Anchors are not the place to cut corners. If you can't afford to equip the route safely and properly, it is not the time to put up the route.

Left to Right: Chains, Cold Shuts, Quick-Links, and Rap Rings

Fixed Anchor Set-Ups

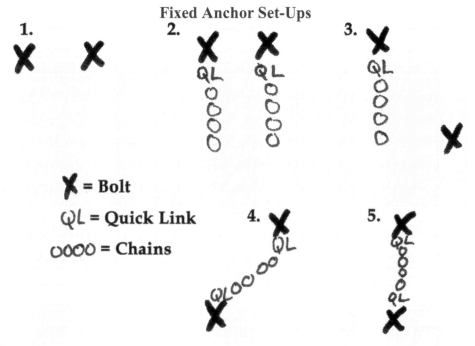

Shown Above

1. Side by side large diameter smooth edge rappel bolts (Metolius rappel bolts) or Cold Shuts. 2. Side by side bolts and chains. 3. Staggered bolts with a chain to reach the lower bolt. 4. Staggered bolts attached by a chain. 5. Vertically oriented bolts connected by a chain. The rappel point in the figures above can be either through a rap ring, quick-link, or a Metolius-style rappel hanger.

It can become very satisfying to equip or re-equip a climbing area with quality and safe equipment. It should be viewed as a community service if the job is done right. Educate yourself, inform yourself, and get out there to gain the experience needed. Some people just never seem to get it, as there are plenty of poor bolt placements and pathetic belay stations even from "experienced" climbers. But seek excellence in whatever you do. Persevere, Adapt, and Overcome. Quality, after all, offers its own rewards.

Fixe Ring Anchor

Side by side bolts are ok in solid rock and where organization at the belay is helpful. Vertically oriented bolts create less total force, and therefore are the strongest anchor. However, the quality of the surrounding rock will dictate the optimal placement. If your set-up involves rappelling from a single point such as in #4 or #5, make sure you use a beefy quick-link, ring, or a steel carabineer.

In Switzerland, the popular set up is drilling two vertically placed bolts with hangers with the upper one at about a 2 o'clock position from the lower one (as in #4 above). Then with quick-links on both ends of a single link of chain, connect them. Finally from the lower bolt, attach a steel carabineer or large quick-link (at least ½") with a rap ring. This is similar to the popular Fixe chain to a ring anchor (shown below).

Chris at the Uintah Mountain crag climbs of Utah likes to place vertically placed bolts (as in #5 above). One piece of 5 or 7 link 3/8" or ½" chain connected by quick-link to the hanger (so they can be replaced periodically) extending down to equalize another ring hanger (such as those available by Fixe shown below).

Jason from Maple Canyon likes to use side by side ring bolts which are also fine (as in #1 above). The only drawback with this system is that it does twist the rope while pulling and could potentially complicate retrieving your rope on multiple rappels.

REMOVING BOLTS

Before you remove a bolt that's not yours, make sure you have permission from the first ascenionist or a general consensus from the local climbing community. First try and remove the entire bolt by using a funkness device or a hammer with chain attached. You can try prying it out with a big crowbar as well. If the bolt won't come out a hammer and chisel may be used to shear the end of the bolt off of the rock. You can also use the blade end of a piton as well. Try not to scar the rock, and find a suitable place to replace the bolt or anchor. Most anchors only need the chain replaced. Don't replace anchors with webbing or rope, please!

ROPE SOLOING

Rope soloing is a great way to get out when a partner can't be found. It is more labor intensive and you'll probably want to lower your lead level a bit, but after practice it can be just as quick and safe as climbing with a partner. The major drawback is that you must find bomber anchors with an upwards direction of pull for each belay, and you must rappel each pitch and jug back up to clean it (unless you're just climbing a ½ a pitch).

You must have some sort of device attached to your harness to catch you if you fall. Commercial devices like the Silent Partner, Soloist, and Solo Aid are available. The Silent Partner is the only device that will hold an upside-down fall and is highly recommended. You can rig auto locking devices like a Petzl Gri-Gri, but they are not sold for solo climbing. The lead rope you use must be the recommended size for the solo belay device you own. Generally speaking, a 10mm rope with a little fuzz on it works best. Skinny new ropes can zip right through. All but the clove hitch and Silent Partner require a Chest Harness to prevent an upside-down fall and improve rope feed.

Luckily, there is a simple system you can use that doesn't require extra gear: the clove hitch. Tie a clove hitch in the lead rope into a solid locking carabiner attached to your harness (through your belt and leg loop like you would with tying into the lead rope – not into the belay loop). As you climb, you loosen the clove hitch and slide it up the rope. Sound tedious? It is indeed, which is why the other mechanical devices are quite popular. You can use two biners with clove hitches tied separated by enough slack to make a few moves, however. The clove hitch system is really best for self-rescue situations.

The system for rope soloing is actually pretty simple. Attach the end of the rope to an anchor with an upwards and outwards direction of pull. To be safe, have it have a downwards direction of pull unless the ground would stop you before that even mattered. Use solid biners and knots, and it doesn't hurt to add screamers or load limiters to the system. To do this, fix the end of the rope to the anchor as usual. Now clip a load limiter to the anchor as well and fix it to the rope just above the end of the rope (with a bit of slack). It is up to you whether you tie into the other end of the climbing rope. If all else fails, this will keep you attached to the anchor, but if you'd hit the ground anyways or you completely trust your back-up knot and self-belay gizmo then don't bother tying in. Attach the solo device on the rope leading just above the anchor with one or two locking carabiners. Now start climbing and placing gear as you normally would, being careful which of the many lines hanging off your harness you clip. If you fall (and the device holds) you should fall onto your gear and the rope will pull up on the anchor, stopping your fall. If you can't get back on the wall, it is important to carry ascenders with you. ***Shown: Weight attached to anchor (haul bag) to provide a dynamic belay. Dotted line represent increased fall distance when bag lifts up.***

One way to soften the fall is to attach something heavy to the anchor tie in point like a haul bag. When you fall, the heavy object will be lifted up before the anchor comes tight, reducing the impact force of the fall. Impact forces of rope soloing are greater than a human belay. The only drawback with weighting the anchor is it increases your fall potential by however long the anchor slings are.

YOU MUST TIE BACKUP KNOTS IN THE ROPE TO PROTECT YOU IF THE SOLO DEVICE SHOULD FAIL. Tie one to three on the ground in places on the rope where you think you may need them. Many folks just use one back-up knot and re-tie it when they reach the knot. You can tie a figure-8 on a bight, or a clove hitch (easier to untie while leading) onto a locking carabineer and clip that into your tie in point as well. Your tie in point may have up to 2-5 locking carabineers in it, but this is the price for safety and not having friends to climb with. When you climb to the point in the rope with a back-up knot, unclip and untie the knot and keep climbing, making sure there is at least one back-up knot in the system. Back-up knots also keep the weight of the rope off of your solo device, causing easier feeding.

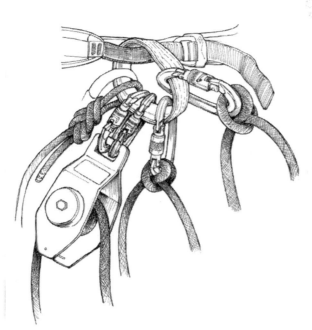

Safest Setup Shown Above: Silent Partner attached to belay look with two locking biners, the end of the rope tied in, and two backup clove hitches on lockers spaced 50 feet apart

Since this whole system is backwards from normal leading (where the leader ties into the end of the rope, not just above the rope tied to the anchor in a normal lead set-up) there will be a nice coil of rope at the anchor. If this looks like it will be a problem (if the rope gets snarled, or caught) you can make a rope bucket out of a large stuff sack with some material you sew or glue to the outside to stiffen it up. You can also use a rope hook or loop of webbing and carry the rope coil up with you. A light painter's bucket could also do the job, but it is harder to pack.

Another problem with rope soloing is that after you climb high enough, slack begins to develop in the system, thus increasing your fall potential. To fix this problem, climb until the slack begins to be an issue. Put a piece of gear in and clip it to the rope as usual. Now, tie a prusik made from easily breakable shoelace (or similar) string and clip it to the piece of gear with a easily breakable keychain carabineer. The prusik will hold the rope up and get rid of the slack, but since it's so breakable, it won't be part of the system. Using a regular prusik and carabineer would cause too much shock in the system if you fell onto it.

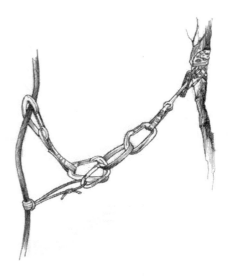

Right: Breakable prusik and biner attached to the rope.

If the pitch was less than half a rope length, you can just rap down the free end. If the pitch was longer, you will need two ropes. I use a static line for my 2nd rope. Rap down, clean the anchor, and jug back up on your ascenders and etriers. If the pitch doesn't lend itself to jugging, or you want to re-climb it, the Silent Partner can be used to top-rope as well. You can also use a rope-clamp like the Petzl Shunt, or use your ascender as a back-up and slide it up as you climb. Just be sure to ALWAYS TIE BACK-UP KNOTS IN THE ROPE WHEN JUGGING OR RE-CLIMBING THE PITCH. Tie a figure-8 on a bight on the rope you are re-climbing to your tie-in point with enough distance to catch a fall without hitting a ledge or the ground. Before you unclip from a back-up knot, tie a new one and clip into that first! When you jug back to the anchor, begin the process again if it's a multipitch route. Practice rope soloing with a back-up belay to double check your systems and to make sure your solo belay device will hold a fall.

Silverstar Peak, WA

GRADES, PARTNERS, AND MENTAL GAMES

To get better, go cragging and lead at or above your limit. Top roping will only take you so far. Take falls on your gear and become quick at French freeing through the hard spots. You have to become comfortable falling to speed up your leading ability. A scary fall or piece of gear that rips can permanently spook even the most seasoned climber. The Rock Warrior's Way, by Arno Ilgner is a great book on mental training for climbing.

A crack is a crack is a crack. In fact, easier climbs are usually more dangerous to fall on because of the angle and ledges. You own the gear, fall on it. If you can climb 5.8, then get on a 5.9 or 5.10. Don't think about the grade or it will psych you out. Maybe you could lead it or at least follow it if you didn't know it was 5.11? Go to a new area without the guidebook (or keep it hidden until you really need it!) and try climbing cracks or faces that are well protected without knowing the grade. Maybe you'll cruise a 5.11 and you're a 5.9 climber. Ironically enough, you could whimper up a 5.4 since you don't know what the grade is! Don't be discouraged if a route is really hard and you thought you could lead a 5.11 but you just got completely spanked on a 10b. 10b's (or 5.7's for that matter) can be way harder than 5.11s. If you want to improve your route finding skills, then don't bring a topo.

With water ice, I'd actually focus on top-roping WI6's and 7's. Can you do a pull-up? Then you can top rope WI6. The more mileage you get ice climbing, the more you'll trust your swings and gear placements - which are the only difference between WI2 and WI6. If you can top-rope a WI6 without falling then you should be able to lead a WI4 after putting one week into leading WI3. After you've led at least 5 pitches of WI4 (and that's real WI4, not fat midseason wet plastic WI4) then get on a WI5. If you lead a few WI5's, then you'll probably lead a WI6 by accident.

For aid, practice dicey aid placement on top-rope, or on lead just above a bolt or super solid piece of gear. 5.10 in the mountains is 5.10 at the crag, and sometimes it's actually easier (5.9 A2, however, is not).

Sport climbers can improve their grade by "hang-dogging" routes (taking on almost every bolt). Stick clipping helps you get up something above your grade as well, since the focus is on the climbing, not the danger of leading. Another way of getting the rope up there on a route with pre-placed draws is to take a large loop of rope, and twirl it around really fast until it snaps into the hanging draw. Using chalk to "tick" holds is an excellent trick to help you find the best holds for your redpoint attempt. Climbing on colder days increases the co-efficient of friction, thus making rubber "stickier". Redpointing (attempting a route on lead multiple times until you climb it without handing or falling) can get boring, but is essential to becoming a better sport climber. Bouldering is another way to help your lead grade improve. Go with someone who knows the moves and can coach you along on the harder problems.

Learn from your failures. What went wrong? Were you blaming something else when really you were just scared or not willing to commit? Commit! You either go up or down. If you're going up, be confident that you can deal, even if it starts becoming miserable. At least go up *one* more pitch, or at least a few feet above your gear. You can rappel and hike out in the rain so try and push on regardless of the weather.

Discipline is the key to success and avoiding epics. Eat and drink even if you don't want to. Add or remove a layer instead of overheating or getting cold. Trust your choices and stick with it! Laziness and shortcuts will lead to failure or disaster.

Make sure your partner isn't going to bag out on you. Look for warning signs…slowing down… excessive looking around…sighing…stopping for extended periods of time on the hike when you're not tired, or on the route when it's not that bad. Partners are by far the number one reason for not getting up something. If you drove all this way just to have a nice hike in the hills, why did you buy all that stuff, lug it around, and probably make lots of sacrifices to do so? You didn't, so get up it and, quit complaining about it being cold or wet or hard or scary. It takes real skill to make these calls, and there are consequences for pushing on, so be honest with yourself: are you in danger, or do you not want to be uncomfortable now, or tired at work tomorrow?

Having your climbing day on a Sunday, or the day before you start work again is a motivation killer, and is a huge reason why people wind up bailing. I realize there's not a lot you can do about this, but know it's a factor before you head out. Have everything ready for the next week so all you have to do when you get home from the climb is go to sleep and go to work (sometime it's going directly to work!)

I highly recommend investing in a "Silent Partner" belay device or rigging up a Gri Gri for rope soloing. Not only will you get out a ton more, you'll also become a much quicker climber. If you think your partner may bail, tell them a story about a partner who bailed for being a total sissy. This reverse psychology could work on your weak-bail-minded partner. If your partner bails on you without ample time to find another partner, it is well within your rights to make them feel awful and pay for everything on the next trip. If they do this three times to you, dump them and find a more reliable partner.

Above: Davis Peak, WA
Below: Spectre Peak, WA

Chapter Five: Gear

Ancient Art, UT

The following is a gear list for a long day climb to a multiday alpine climb. Single pitch craggers and boulderers can glean some information from this section by reading about various types of gear. You may be able to climb a route totally naked - the point is that all items are optional so go over everything to see if you really need to bring it. Bring what you need to get up and down the route as quickly and safely as possible. If you are sleeping on the route, be extra picky about what goes in the pack and be willing to suffer a bit more. Casual hikes to a base camp could contain comforts not included in this list. If this is the case, pack it all! Lots of alpinists pack like they are going for a one day push up a hard route when they go car camping!

To reduce weight, start with the heaviest single item. Start with your pack, tent, or sleeping bag and work your way down. See what you can kill two birds with –your cook pot can also be your bowl and mug. Your garbage can also be your pot-holder. Be creative! Your bivy kit should be only slightly more comfortable than a forced open bivy. You need to plan on one emergency bivy/day out for longer trips - which usually means packing~600 extra calories. Make a copy of this list and tape it up in your gear closet. Force your partner to check the list before you get in the car.

Never assume your partner has something, and if they say "they got it" and it's something you're picky about, make sure they do indeed "got it." Maybe they were supposed to bring breakfast and they don't drink coffee and you do. These are things to find out. If they get annoyed by your constant phone calls and emails checking in on this stuff, they are going to be a bad partner anyways.

CAMPING AND APPROACHING

BACKPACKS
Approach Pack
Really try to get everything inside a lightweight 45 Liter pack for a multi-day or winter climb. Get one that is essentially frameless with a foam pad to create the frame. Cilogear makes a 45L pack that weights one pound and is very durable. I managed to pack 8 days worth of food and gear into one for a 1st ascent in the summer-time.

> *You can use your sleeping pad as the frame and remove all excess slings, clips, etc…from the pack, including the pack lid if need be.*

Lightweight Summit Pack (with durable keychain or ultralight biner for clipping to the anchor)
This may be worth the extra weight if your approach pack is too big climb with comfortably, especially if you have a base camp. If you're sleeping on the route, this is obviously a useless item. The keychain biner is useful for hanging your pack at the belay. I pre-tie a loop of tat to three strong anchor points on the pack to avoid having a sling from the rack donated to the pack.

> *Try and double your summit pack as your sleeping bag stuff sack.*

Garbage Bags
Helpful to line the bottom of your pack (clothes and bag), and handy in case it will rain hard or you will be bushwhacking in wet weather. If it's too hot to wear your rain jacket when it's raining, you can also put your rain coat over your backpack.

SLEEPING EQUIPMENT
Sleeping Bags
Yes sleeping bags are optional. Bring a 20 to 40 degree 800+ fill down bag for dry weather or a synthetic bag for extended wet weather (why are you out in that weather?) with a lightweight shell material. If you sleep warm, get a 40 degree bag for summertime use. If you sleep cold, don't skimp too much because a bad night's sleep will cost the climb.

If your belay jacket is warm enough and you think you'll be warm enough, consider buying a half-bag. Feathered Friends and Nunatak Gear make excellent down half-bags. If it's a matter of weight, there are double sleeping bags such as the Feathered Friends "Spoonbill". Another option is to have a triangular piece of nylon sewn with male and female zipper ends on each side. This can turn one bag into a two person bag.

A zero degree down bag is acceptable for most winter climbs, but use synthetic fill if it's a multi day or at least greater than a two night trip – especially if you're moving your camp site multiple times or it's going to be damp out. If you are careful it is possible to keep a down bag dry. Epic or Pertex fabric sleeping bag covers are necessary to keep condensation off down bags in winter or wet weather.

Down Bag with Epic Bag Cover

Sleeping Bag Compression Sack
Ones made out of silicone nylon (or use your summit pack) are useful to create more space in your pack. Pack this in your bag second, just after you put your water bladder in. No other stuff sacks are needed unless you have super light tiny ditty bag to organize little stuff like lip balm, alarm clocks, etc inside the tent (or use your pack lid).

Sleeping Pad and Pillow

Ultra-light Therm-a-rests are just about the warmest choice, but they are still kind of heavy and can deflate or puncture. Ridge Rests (good) Z-Rests (better), or yellow closed cell foam "hardman" pads (best but most uncomfortable) keep the ground from making you cold. These closed cell foam pads are nice because you can use them around camp to lie on. Ridge Rests and Z-Rests pads trap snow, so be aware. The great thing about Z-Rests are their durability and light weight. You don't have to baby them, and you can toss them around camp for sitting or gear organizing.

Ropes make great pillows, as do water bladders with a piece of clothing over them to insulate. Mont-Bell makes a very light air pillow that is worth the weight on multi-day trips.

Use the rope for your pad if you're going super light. Don't bother getting a long pad - use your empty pack as the bottom 3rd of your pad. You can even put your legs inside the pack if need be.

SHELTER
Tents, Tarps and Bivy Sacks
Black Diamond Betalight or the Firstlight/Lighthouse style single wall silicone nylon tents or tarps are extremely lightweight, mostly waterproof, and are very easy to set-up. You have to pitch your tarp on a ground surface that will absorb water during heavy rain, however. Brooks-Range equipment unveiled an unwoven dyneema tent that has your trecking poles and avy probe designed into the tent design. It only weights a pound! Bivy sacks are only necessary if it's too steep to pitch a tent on route and it may rain.

Use your trekking poles instead of the poles provided for the Firstlight tent if you're not worried about your tent blowing down, and use your helmet or climbing shoes to protect the fabric if you're using the Firstlight tent.

Wayne Wallace Photo

Above: Bugaboos, Canada

Single wall waterproof-breathable tents such as the Bibler are better for longer trips in severe weather. Double wall tents are the most waterproof, least prone to condensation, but a much heavier that the other shelters mentioned. Put your sleeping pads and backpacks UNDER the tent to protect the floor fabric.

Snow Shelters
Snow caves are the shelter of choice on long winter routes and only require a shovel blade to make. If you have time, you can make a Quinsy in the winter.

To make a Quinsy, pile up a huge mound of packable snow, pack it down and wait a bit for the snow to settle then hollow out the snow mound. To build a snow cave on a slope, first dig the entrance in three feet. The main living area should be above the entrance, so angle up after three feet and hollow out a large enough area to sleep and cook. You need a minimum of one foot thickness for the ceiling. Poke out a ventilation hole at a diagonal away from where you'll be sleeping. Smooth out the walls of the cave to. When making the cave try to wear as little clothing under your shell as possible to avoid getting soaking wet.

Tent Stakes
Use four of the cheap thin types. Find rocks for the rest of the stakes. Use your poles, axes, and other assorted gear you won't use during the climb. In winter, use the U shaped snow stakes. You can also bury sticks, stuff sacks, or pretty much anything for your tent stakes.

COOKING EQUIPMENT
Stove
Use an MSR Pocket Rocket or similar canister gas stove, or use a white gas Whisperlight stove for summer use if you do not require melting snow for water. MSR Reactor (for shorter trips) or MSR XGK stoves (for longer trips) are great for winter.

Windscreen
Doubled-up aluminum foil is cheaper and lighter than commercial windscreens

Fuel
I almost always go with canister (propane) gas unless I'm climbing a multiday winter route. For one to two nights bring a smaller canister for one to two people. For three nights bring a large canister. In winter bring a 125ml of propane per person per day. White gas stoves use about 4oz gas per person per day and in winter the use 8oz white gas per person per day.

1-1.5 Liter Aluminum Pot.
Barely heavier than titanium, aluminum conducts heat much better. Bring a lid to reduce heating time. Creating a hanging stove out of an MSR Reactor stove and pot is really easy. Don't use pot grips: use garbage or your sleeves. I use two pots with my partner, one slightly larger than the other. The larger fits upside-down over the smaller pot and acts as a lid and bowl. Neither person brings a bowl, and we re-use the packaging from a freeze dried meal for eating out of.

Heat Exchangers
I think these are a waste of weight. The best use for a heat exchanger is to keep your butane cartage from freezing. To do this, make a closed-cell foam cozy for your gas canister.

Jet Boil and Reactor stoves both have built in heat exchangers. But to keep the propane warm enough to work on any canister-style store, take some flat wide 1/8inch wide copper wire and wrap it around the canister, leaving enough tail to poke up into the flame. Also, put the canister on a non-conductive surface like your sleeping pad, or use a shovel blade.

Bowl and Cup
If you must have a hot drink, bring a 16 to 32oz plastic measuring cup or use your Nalgene so you can make your breakfast in the pan while drinking your hot drink (or see my system above under the pot section). Just don't waste time sipping your hot drink from your Nalgene if you will be re-filling it with water for the climb that morning. Go over your bowl, cup, and pot plan with your partner beforehand to avoid bringing extra items. There are a lot of lightweight bowl/cup items on the market. The latest rage is "squishy" silicone collapsible cups that pack down easily and weigh less than a plastic counterpart. The lightest, most packable item I've seen besides a paper bowl (which last a surprisingly long time) are flat plastic origami dish sets.

2 Tiny Lighters
Carry one in your toilet paper bag, and don't forget to pack it in your summit pack just in case (you never know where you may wind up - seriously). Carry the other in your mess kit.

Spoon
Spoons are nice. If you've got the money, a titanium spoon is light and is good for digging up snow for meltwater. Better yet, grab a plastic spoon from the hamburger joint you ate at on the drive in. Pitons and nut tools make excellent spoons. Ski to Summit gear makes the lightest spoon that won't break I've ever seen. It comes with a hyper-light titanium carabineer you can put on your camera bag.

HYDRATION
Water Bladders and Containers
100oz Camelback-style bladders are my personal favorite. The soft rubber doesn't crack, and the wide mouth makes filling it easier. Aluminum bottles like Sigg are popular, but I'm not a fan. Duct-taping a cheap water bottle with a lightweight sling (in case you need it for gear) you can clip to your harness is a good way to climb shorter climbs in summer. Two one-liter Nalgene style bottles with bottle parkas are better suited for winter. The drinking tube on a hydration system will freeze and make it impossible to drink. I haven't seen an insulated system that actually works. Also, Nalgene-style water bottles can be used to make hot water bottles for your sleeping bag at night.

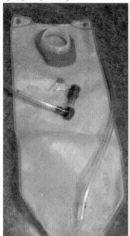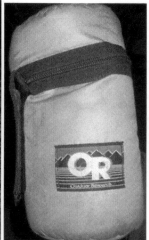

Water Purification
Chlorine drops and tablets are quick and potent, although the bottle can leak. Both the drops and the tablets take four hours to kill <u>everything</u>. Iodine pills are ok, but don't kill as many microbes. Save weight by taking as many chlorine tablets as you think you may need. Filters and steri pens are useless except for getting water out of desert potholes, or on International expeditions. Or go for it and drink it straight from the source natural style! If in doubt, go with the drops.

Straw
A straw is handy for quick water breaks, or for sucking on trickles while climbing.

BIVY AND RESCUE KIT

Take some, none, or all of the items mentioned – it's up to you. Some items have or will already be mentioned in this text. Shown here are a few hydrocodone pills (wrapped in tin foil and cardboard - beg your M.D. for a prescription), a small roll of athletic tape, a smaller role of duct tape (roll it around a thin pencil, your gas bottle, or your hiking poles – just remember to change it frequently), sleeping pills (in the form of allergy pills shown), nail clippers, crazy glue, Tiblock / Ropeman, tat material, mini led headlamp, knife (if it's not on my nut tool), iodine tablets (take a few and wrap them in tin foil to save weight), chlorine tablets, toilet paper, hand warmers, lip balm, blister pads, ear plugs, emergency bivy blanket, fire starting tablets, small lighter, alarm clock, cell phone, NSAIDs, I-pod, and a map and compass.

Not shown but quite useful are, a GPS, a high-calorie energy bar (Pemmican Bars pack a wallop), a partner who can run really fast, and a tiny handheld video game (I have no idea what's systems or games are good), and the fifi hook / rubber band rope retrieval set-up. Some of these items are nice to keep in the zipper pocket of your chalk bag for easy access.

MODES OF TRAVEL
Trekking Poles
Get cheap ones because you'll break them. Lightweight expensive ones are great if you can afford to replace them. Wal-Mart sells trekking poles for around ten dollars. Trekking poles are usually necessary to set up tarps. The poles are annoying to store in the pack while climbing, however. Poles are pretty necessary for snowy winter travel.

Trekking poles can be used as your ice-ax if you are savvy and daring, as well as tent stakes, or a hasty picket.

Snowshoes vs. Skis vs. Boot Packing
Bring skis if you think you can ski down what you skinned up, or prepare to carry them. Skis are usually the fastest way up, but can be slower on the way down if there are lots of trees or if you suck at skiing. Snowshoes are your other option for really deep snow. They are miserable to use, so walk a bit from to car to see if you actually need them. Snowshoes are also much lighter to carry if you have to put them on your pack. I think skis work best on logging roads and glaciers, and boots are the best on trails if you can get away without using snowshoes.

Mt. Rainier, WA

GLACIER AND AVALANCHE GEAR

Shovel.
One shovel should do. See if your ice tool fits in the head to save weight. Shovels can save hours if you have to dig a snow cave or tunnel through a cornice. They also make nice deadman anchors in soft snow.

Wands
Only use these if the way up is also the way down, the forecast is poor, there are lots of crevasses, or you can't find your way down because the route is complex. They are very useful in marking where a food cache or the latrine is, or on flat glaciated terrain near your camp in case of a white-out. Just be sure not to leave them as litter on the mountain.

Avy Kit: **Beacon, Shovel, Probe**
Necessary to find a buried partner our yourself in avy terrain. Make sure your partner knows how to use his or her beacon and the batteries are fresh. Avy probes make excellent tent poles (and stick clips!)

SUNDRIES

Camera
Put your camera inside a slim neoprene case and clipped with a durable keychain biner. There tiny lightweight camcorders available as well. Video makes a much more interesting slideshow!

Shades
Cheap wrap-around glasses with UVA and B protection are all you really need. Make little duct-tape side shields for snow travel. Goggles are useful for navigating winter storms or on longer mountaineering expeditions.

Sunscreen
Bring just a little travel size tube, and try to bring exactly the amount you plan on using.

Lip Balm
Unless you want everything you eat or drink after the climb to burn, stash a tube in your pocket. I prefer the squeezable tube to the sticks.

Compass, GPS, Altimeter, and Map
ALWAYS bring a watch with digital altimeter, a small no frills compass (an inclinometer is as fancy as you should get), and a map. Bring one topo each. Don't trust your digital compass. If you bring a GPS, you still must bring a real compass and map. Suunto makes a watch with GPS, compass, altimeter, and barometer built in.

Loud Travel Alarm Clock
Only if you need it.

Ear Plugs
An absolute lifesaver and super light. Bring an extra set for your partner who will probably forget them, lose sleep, and want to bail in the morning. Don't sleep past the alarm!

Sleeping Pills
You must sleep to perform, so pack a couple just in case. Try them out at home first to make sure they work for you. See the nutrition section for more details.

Travel Toothbrush and Paste
If it's one night, pre-paste it or just skip it altogether. "Brush-ups" are super light disposable fingertip tooth brushes. They don't do a very good job, but are better than nothing.

Toilet Paper
REI and Wal-Mart sell tightly pre-rolled little packages that last a four day trip. Keep your spare lighter with this in a small light zip lock. In winter just use snow and have some scrap T.P. for "spotting"

Bug Dope
100% DEET is great for mosquitoes, or a blend for other no-see-ums. Permethrin spray on your clothes and non-climbing gear pre-trip really helps a lot.

A great trick to keep the mosquitoes at bay is to lay down when your partner and you are taking a rest break. Mosquitoes seem to attack the person who is higher up!

Headlamp
Bring a tiny micro L.E.D light if you think you won't need to route find, otherwise bring it anyway and stash it in your back or chalk bag. Otherwise get something with a super-bright L.E.D and normal led combo. Unless it's a really long trip don't bring extra batteries, but spend the cash and get fresh ones before the climb.

I-pod
Awesome if your partner is annoying, the approach is epic, or for forced bivy entertainment. Bring a dual earphone splitter so you and your tent mate can both listen to a movie. Bring some tiny rubber bands to rig up your home theater.

Solar Charger
Several lightweight options exist to solar charge your camera, gps, ipod, etc on longer expeditions. Lighter than a bunch of batteries. Solio makes the lightest and cheapest model. For i-pod recharging, buy a battery booster. They are very light and allow you plenty of power for "movie nights" in the tent.

Book
Extra weight but nice if there's a lot of time to kill in camp. Tear out a page for your partner to read so you both don't have to bring one. Use it as T.P., pot-grips, or a fire-starter. Bring a notebook and pen instead of a book to start your life's memoirs.

Piss bottle
Priceless. A wide mouth platypus (the size depends on you) is perfect.

Lady-J or Freshette
For the female climber. These devices allow females to urinate with their harnesses on. Clip it to your pack or harness in a little mesh ditty bag so it dries out and is handy.

CLOTHING

FOOTWEAR

Approach Shoes

Sandals, tennis shoes, or lightweight approach shoes are all you need for summer unless you have really bad ankles: this includes easy glacier travel or soft steep snow during the summer months! Always seam seal the heck out of your approach shoes a few times before you use them. A few trips and soggy conditions can ruin a pair of expensive approach shoes in less than a season. The market is in bad need of a great pair of approach shoes. One of the best ever was the old Nike Air Cider Cone (no longer available). The best pair I've used since are the Five Ten Insights, mostly for their stickiness and lack of seams. Seams on approach shoes come apart like crazy, no matter how much you Seam Grip them. Also, the heels on most approach shoes seem to get chewed up very quickly. I pre-duct tape the heels with strong glue (shiny side out of course).

If you get blisters or haven't worn your shoes before, bring along a bit of duct tape to prevent blisters. You can also try rubbing body glide on your heel or the bottom of your foot to reduce friction (body glide is also nice for between your legs or on your chest if you suffer from excessive rubbing in those areas). You can't do duct-tape and body glide on top of each other since the tape won't stick. Sometimes the heel of the shoe gets chewed up. In this case, I superglue enforce duct-tape to the heel of my shoe for permanent damage control. Another common cause of blisters is sweat. If this is the case, antiperspirant is strong enough for your feet (but made for your armpits).

Camp Shoes

It's nice to have a pair of very light flip-flops, sandals, or felt karate-style slippers for camp. Sandals are great for crossing streams and will dry out by camp, but are hard to walk around in with socks on.

Climbing Shoes

Make sure your climbing shoes are comfy for longer routes, but tight enough for harder climbing. Mythos are my favorite for almost every type of rock climbing. The more diversified you climbing, the more shoes you'll wind up owning. Barracudas were another great all-around trad shoe, but sadly they no longer exist.

Lightweight climbers: I have found that if you weigh less than, let's say, 150lbs, board lasted shoes are not in the cards for you because smearing will be difficult. I wore board lasted Ace's and Kaukulators for years before I realized this – any my climbing improved drastically. Don't do a long route in a new pair of shoes!

Ice Boots

Make sure your boots fit! See the approach shoe section for info on blister control. Single leather or synthetic boots are generally the best for all ice routes, or for one to two nights out. Double boots are necessary for multi-day trips or very cold conditions. Fruit boots (boots with crampons permanently attached) are really nice for one pitch close to the road ice climbing

You can make your own fruit boots by drilling the front and back sections of your old crampons onto a pair of lightweight boots.

Insulated Overboots can drastically increase the warmth of your ice boots, especially your leathers. The drawback is that you must always wear your crampons with these. Get them tight, and don't get the insulated supergaiters because they only insulate the tops of your feet and lower leg. A thin layer of closed cell foam cut to fit your footbed can help from the conductive heat loss from the bottom of your shoes.

Socks
Bring 2nd pair if it's an overnight (hoard that other pair!). Lightweight merino wool or thin synthetic types work well. Don't try out any new socks (or boots and shoes) for a long approach! Some companies make a double layer sock to reduce friction between your foot and the shoe. I can swear by these! I prefer the thinnest sock possible when approaching in the summer. I bring two pair (one for the hike in and one for the hike out). I also bring a 3rd, warmer pair that I stash inside my sleeping bag and only wear at camp in my camp shoes. In winter, a pair of the thickest merino wool socks you can find are your best option. Bring at least two pairs if it's an overnight.

Gaiters
Don't bother with Gore-Tex gaiters. If you are wearing gaitors then chances are you already have a shell on under them. So why have two layers of Gore-Tex on top of one another? Thin nylon or soft-shell materials work just fine. Find the lowest profile that will fit over your boot. I don't recommend any gaitors for summer use. Pebbles will eventually find their way in, and your feet will overheat and get sweaty. Plus you'll look like a total dork. Outdoor Research still makes the best gaitors.

Vapor Barrier Liners (or bread bags) worn over thin liner socks help keep your outer socks dry and your feet warmer. If sweating is a major issue with the vapor barrier socks, you can try rubbing antiperspirant on your feet. I do not recommend the trick of putting cayenne pepper on your feet to aid in warmth. The drawbacks far outweigh any warmth you may supposedly get from this.

Another trick is to put shake and warm heat packs in your socks at night (and in your sleeping bag) to help dry things out. Hot packs inside the boot while wearing them usually get way to hot and you lose any gained heat when your feet start sweating (unless it's just ridiculously cold outside).

HEADGEAR
Warm Hat
In addition to a warm wool or fleece hat to bring around year long, add a balaclava for winter if conditions warrant. Avoid buying Windstopper hats because it is very difficult to hear through the wind stopper membrane.

Ball cap
So you don't burn your bald spot and to keep the sun out of your eyes.

Bandana or Sun Hat
Good for sleeping to protect against mosquitoes, for neck burns, general camp use, and showin' your colors to the other camp homies. Outdoor Research makes a ball-cap with a snap-on neck bandana. You'll look stupid but anyone that hates the sun as much as summertime alpinists will really appreciate the protection. Spray it with Permethrin to help with bugs.

Wayne WallacePhoto

188

HANDWEAR

Gloves

Don't bother in the summer unless there is glacier travel, snow climbing involved, or your hands get cold really easily. For any of the above reasons, bring a light pair or just liners. In the winter you want a glove combo that one pair is dexterous and just warm enough for climbing, and another pair is a little bit warmer for belaying and as a back-up. Bring at least two pairs because one will get wet and cold. Keep your used cold wet gloves stuffed in your jacket to warm them during the belay. Bring expedition mitts if you have really poor circulation for climbing, or for walking or belaying if it'll be very cold and snowy. Dry tool gloves are nice for mixed climbing and warm weather belaying. Wind stopper fabric makes an excellent base layer glove. Bring a pair of leather gloves for jumaring, or extensive belaying / rappelling.

Hand Warmers

Bring one for every 8 hours climbing, and 2 for each night if it's going to be really cold. Store them in your chest pocket or with your damp gloves while climbing. If it's not going to be that cold out you can do without them. I almost always forget to bring these!

Find a thin spandex or barely insulated balaclava, cut out the face section, and sew it to the collar of your climbing jacket for a spindrift collar that won't overheat.

Bald Eagle makes just about the best pair of ice climbing gloves I've used. They go for $14 at the local gas station.

LOWER BODY

Durable nylon pants or zip-off pants, or lightweight soft shell pants are nice to block wind and sharp plants. Polypro bottoms are not necessary except for winter climbing - even for camp unless you get really cold. Legs typically don't get too cold. Shorts over poly-pro is a mountain fashion no-no. Soft-shell pants look hip and shed snow well, but they are water sponges.

The pair of underwear you hike in will keep you alive without needing extra pairs. Silk weight underwear is the underwear of choice for keeping the stank down for multiple days. In winter, underwear isn't very necessary because your leggings act the part.

In winter, light or medium weight polypro under a pair of soft-shell bibs (or soft-shell pants with suspenders) is a great option in all but soaking conditions. If you're going to be plowing through snow all day or it's quite wet out try a pair of 200 weight Polartech (like expedition weight Patagonia) stretchy fleece pants with low profile form fitting Gore-Tex pants or bibs as the shell.

One piece polypro suits are great since your pants don't ride up on you creating cold spots and chaffing. For long climbs without lots of places to stop, make sure you can poop without taking your harness off. You'll need either a through the crotch zipper on your bibs, or a harness with leg loops that come totally undone.

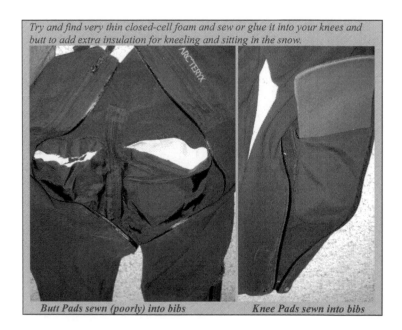

Try and find very thin closed-cell foam and sew or glue it into your knees and butt to add extra insulation for kneeling and sitting in the snow.

Butt Pads sewn (poorly) into bibs   *Knee Pads sewn into bibs*

UPPER BODY

Use a silk weight polypro or lightweight merino wool long sleeve shirt. If it's wicked hot, wear a nylon button-down U.V.- proof shirt, tank top, or cotton t-shirt. Add a mildly insulated windbreaker like the Marmot Dri-Clime model, and a medium weight synthetic jacket (like the Patagonia Puffball) for warmth. If it's going to be a chilly summer, either add a medium weight fleece, or bring a slightly warmer belay jacket in addition. Bring a lightweight rain coat if you would be pretty miserable if it rained on you, or you think it's probably going to rain on the hiking and camping days. If you bring a rain jacket, skip the windbreaker and go with a light fleece.

In winter, start with a medium weight polypro shirt, and add a mildly insulated windbreaker or a tightly woven lightweight soft shell. The tightly woven fabric of the windbreaker creates a vapor barrier (making it warmer and keeping outer layers from getting sweaty) close to your skin. For moving fast or warmer weather, this combo should be enough for hiking and climbing in. If it's really cold, add a fleece sweater and / or a Patagonia Puffball type jacket over the windbreaker (or under the soft shell). Your outer shell should be a Gore-Tex jacket if it's going to be wet or a soft shell jacket preferably with a hood. The last layer in the upper body clothing system is a big puffy belay jacket. A Patagonia DAS parka or similar is warm and stays dry more easily.

If it won't be wet conditions, or it'll be really cold, a big puffy down jacket is warmer for the weight. Alpine ice route belays usually aren't as wet as waterfall routes, but things can get damp while bivying fairly easily. I prefer a gigantic 850 fill down jacket with a highly water resistant (but not water-proof) shell if I can manage to fit it in the pack. To me it is worth the extra weight to be warm during the belay and at camp, unless I expect things to be quite damp.

A note on synthetic vs. wool long underwear, and Windstopper fabrics: one of the biggest drawbacks to wool has been overheating and weight. With recent advances in wool technology (yikes!) companies like Smart Wool have crafted silky smooth and lightweight long underwear that feel just like silk weight polypro. These wool garments do a better job with moisture transport from sweating and stay amazingly cool in hot weather. They are more expensive, however, but are worth looking into. I don't recommend Windstopper fabric for insulated layers or as shell material. Windbreakers, soft-shell jackets, and lightweight rain jackets block the wind equally well, but don't overheat nearly as much. Windstopper works great for gloves or other types of clothing for other activities besides climbing. Remember, Windstopper hats make you unable to hear, overheat, and act like a loudspeaker in your ear if it's windy.

190

CLIMBING EQUIPMENT
HARNESSES AND HELMETS
Helmet

Always wear a helmet! Countless injuries occur from head injuries – even while top roping an easy pitch at a sport crag. Under no circumstance should you place anything firm, or pack something in tightly under your helmet webbing (if your helmet has webbing inside of it). An impact from above would transmit the force through what should have been an empty space, into your head and kill you.

Harness

For longer, more gear intensive route, your harness should have adjustable leg loops, big gear loops, and a haul loop in the back. Lightweight molded harness are perfect for sport or short trad routes.

Petzl makes a helmet with a visor for eye protection while ice climbing which helps avoid the glasses fogging up scenario, and Grivel makes a helmet with a full on cage protecting your face

John Frieh Photo

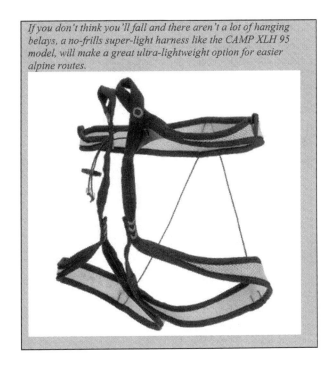

If you don't think you'll fall and there aren't a lot of hanging belays, a no-frills super-light harness like the CAMP XLH 95 model, will make a great ultra-lightweight option for easier alpine routes.

On Your Harness
Keep a 6mm short length of perlon for a rappel autoblock tied with a double fisherman knot and girth hitched several times around a leg loop (see the rappel section).
Keep two free wire gates for anchor management and the inevitable *"where are all the biners?"* question.

You should have one lightweight locker and an ATC-style lightweight belay device (or a baguette for thinner ropes) for belaying. Also, bring a Kong Gi-Gi or Reverso-type auto-locking belay device, another locker, and wire gate for bringing up the 2nd. The weight of this extra device is well worth the time saved during belay change-over (see climbing fast).

Mini-Reverso, Baguette, ATC, and Gi-Gi (bottom)

Also on your harness should be a daisy chain (optional) and lightweight keylock locking biner for the daisy. To save weight, clove hitch directly into the anchor points. This is also safe because your daisy chain isn't meant to hold much of a fall (the Metolius P.A.S. is full strength however). When you're rappelling, you shouldn't be using the free slings, so those can replace your daisy.

Next, keep a nut tool (optional) on a durable key-chain biner or one with a built in clip. Your ice-ax can suffice as a nut tool on winter climbs or alpine climbs requiring one. Kong makes a great lightweight nut tool, and Trango makes one with a built-in knife.

I like to keep a jacket inside a stuff-sack clipped to my harness, and a cheap plastic water-bottle with a sling taped on if I will be climbing without a backpack.

Always have a knife handy. Get one as tiny as you can get, and accessible on your harness – attaching it to your nut-tool or directly to your harness.

> *If you forgot a knife and need to chop the rope grab a rock and bash the rope against the mountain. Use your cams or hammer if there are no loose rocks.*

Bring a 20 foot cordelette (6mm cord or super strong 5mm Kevlar Spectra blend works great) and a locker. Cordelettes are really handy for making quick equalized anchors. 6mm cord is more useful for turning in to tat.

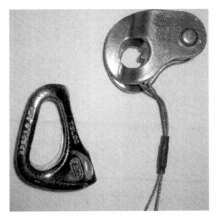

Have a Petzl Tiblock or Wild Country Ropeman (better for smaller ropes) on your harness or in your chalk bag. These are extremely useful to have for jugging or simul-climbing. I keep these and my knife on my nut tool or V-threader biner.

Finally, you can clip a water bottle to your harness in summer if you're not bringing a pack. A cheap plastic with a duct-taped sling and a key-chain biner is the lightest option.

Tibloc (left) Ropeman (right)

For ice routes, keep a V-threader and one length of rappel cord on a durable, light keychain biner for ice routes. You can feed the rope directly through the hole if it's thin enough and your partner does a test pull to make sure it doesn't get frozen in place. You can make a V-threader from a piece of coat hanger with one end sharpened and bent like a hook and the other end twisted up for a carabineer hole. Black Diamond makes a V-threader template in case your aim is off.

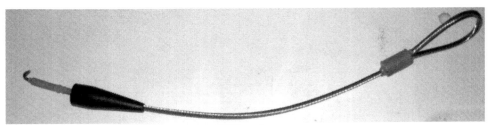

V-Threader

Ice clippers for screws are helpful for steep ice-leads.

****

193

Justin Thibault Photo

SPORT AND BOULDERING PARAPHERNALIA

Brushes
You can buy brushes specifically for climbing, but for the full arsenal you'll want a horse brush and a toothbrush for large and medium-scale cleaning.

Stick Clip
I scoffed at these for years, considering them for sissies. But I wasn't climbing very hard either! If you're out for getting in hard, steep pitches, then a stick clip is a great tool.

Knee Pads
For the true sport connoisseur! Rubber knee pads keep those no hands rest knee bars friendly and pain free. Some sport climbers who specialize in overhanging climbing have multiple sets.

Rope Bag
You can always tell who the alpinists are at the sport crag. If you don't want to be spotted, then bring a rope bag. True sport climbers bring a small square of Astroturf to change their shoes on to protect the soles from slippery dirt.

Lawn Chairs, Mini Cooler, and Propane Heater
Now we are talking. Take a break, eat an actual sandwich (maybe even some fruit or pasta salad), and keep warm while belaying! Actually, the propane heater is pretty sweet for close to the road ice climbing. Bring your thermos of soup and coffee instead of the cooler.

Bouldering Pad
These are actually kind of expensive, but so is the hospital bill for a broken ankle. If you plan on doing much bouldering, it is wise to invest in a commercial bouldering pad. Be careful falling on the sides of pads, especially if two pads are together.

Chalk bag

I like one with a zipper pouch to put sunscreen, clippers, tat, Tiblock, lip balm, headlamp, sleeping pills, a tiny lighter, Vicodin, and crazy glue in. Put the belt through the climbing tape for easy access. Liquid chalk is excellent for a "pre-coat" on the hands for difficult sport-climbing and bouldering.

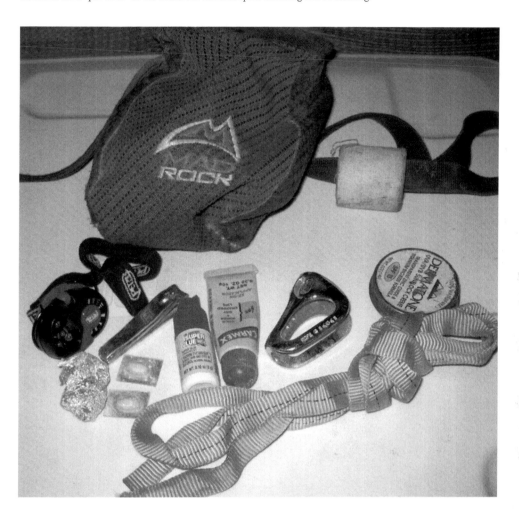

****

ROPES AND SLINGS

Rope

The shorter the rope the lighter the weight, and the longer the rope the longer the pitches and quicker the climbing. 60 meter ropes are still the standard, although 70 meter ropes are gaining popularity. Some rappels are now rigged for 70m ropes only. The nice thing about a 70m rope is that you can get away with bringing just one rope when a 60m just doesn't quite reach the next rappel or belay. Use a 60m rope for standard single rope alpine routes with established pitches (or if you want to shave some weight). If you are in doubt how long pitches are or if you can link them, then go with a 70m. The extra 10 meters can come in very handy. Dry treated ropes are absolutely necessary for winter use, and very handy during summer alpine climbs.

Summer alpine route rope choices:
One 8.9-9.6mm rope is choice if the raps shorter than 30m.

Two 7.7-8.1mm ropes are ideal if there are long raps, the climbing is not extremely difficult, and there aren't a lot of hanging belays (taking in separately clipped ropes and rope management on a hanging belay with twins or half ropes is obnoxious)

One 8.9-9.6mm rope and one 6mm length of perlon of the same length as the lead rope is the lightest option for climbs with double rope rappels and for difficult climbing when you want to go light. The 6mm perlon can also be used for making anchors. A rap line made of spectra/Kevlar can be purchased for maximum security, but it is much more expensive than perlon. If weight isn't a huge issue, use one of your older 8mm ice ropes or a 8mm static haul line as your rappel line instead of a 6mm (the follower can just suffer carrying the heavier load).

Lightweight ropes are great for sending hard sport climbs, but they get trashed very quickly. For cragging, 9.8-10.2mm ropes last the longest with the best handling properties. Aid climbing requires much thicker ropes, especially for jugging and hauling. 11mm ropes are perfect for Aid climbs.

For winter routes with rappels greater than 30 meters, two 7.7 - 8.1mm ropes are usually the best. Otherwise a thin single rope around 8.9 - 9.4mm works well. 70m ropes allow for longer rappels, and finding anchors in winter is more difficult, so I suggest buying 70m ropes for winter use.

Slings

14 total slings, draws, or a combination of the two is a good number for a hard route. I've never heard anyone complain that they brought too many slings up a climb!

Quickdraws

Quickdraws are nice for bolts, steep ice, or for nuts on really hard straight up climbing.

Screamers

Load limiters (Screamers) are essential on ice routes (substitute as many screamers as possible for quick draws on winter climbs), The lightest are the Mammut ultra light screamers. Yates ice and aid screamers don't work for ice because they get caught on your crampons. Standard Yates screamer work fine too. 4-6 for an ice route is a good number.

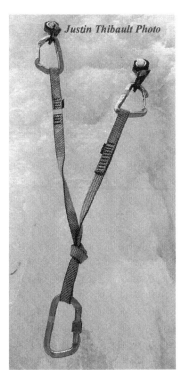

Justin Thibault Photo

Rabbit Runners and Double Length Slings

These are double length pieces of webbing with sewn loops on both ends, and are great substitutes for double length slings. They are lighter, are easier to undo (loop it over your shoulder and remove it without lifting your arm up by just unclipping one end and pulling it out), can be used as anchor equalizers, and can be girth hitched around natural pro more easily. Bring one or two and use one keylock biner per. Double length slings serve the same purpose as rabbit runners, and are essentially sewn slings twice a long as regular slings. I usually bring one rabbit runner / double length sling on an alpine climb, two on alpine ice routes, and none on most cragging routes.

Shoulder Length Slings

These should be the majority of your slings on long or wandering routes. On moderate climbs, half the slings you bring should have one biner each, the other half you can double up with two biners each. If you're climbing difficult terrain, go ahead and keep two biners doubled up on each. You'll need two biners on each sling for ice climbs as well.

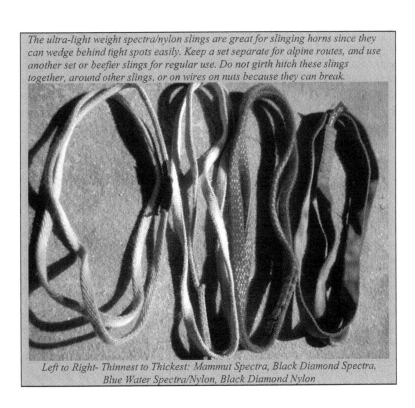

The ultra-light weight spectra/nylon slings are great for slinging horns since they can wedge behind tight spots easily. Keep a set separate for alpine routes, and use another set or beefier slings for regular use. Do not girth hitch these slings together, around other slings, or on wires on nuts because they can break.

Left to Right- Thinnest to Thickest: Mammut Spectra, Black Diamond Spectra, Blue Water Spectra/Nylon, Black Diamond Nylon

Gear Sling

With a larger rack, a gear sling speeds up the belay change-overs and keeps the rack well organized for leading. The 2nd can use a shoulder length sling that he or she cleaned on their way up even if you rack on your harness to lead. I like to use a thick shoulder length sling instead of a commercial gear sling because the commercial slings always rotate around and I wind up trying to unclip my key piece of gear through two inches of padding.

Tat

Always bring tat (scrap rappel webbing). Even a little piece tied to your chalk bag is handy when sport climbing. Supertape is thinner than $9/16^{th}$ inch webbing (used for tying hooks in aid climbing) but it's hard to find. Don't use supertape as sling material! 5-6mm perlon works well too, but thin webbing is nice because you can slide it in under tiny cracks under boulders or horns for rappelling. I've burned through over 200' of tat on a single descent, so bring around ten feet just in case and prepare to leave your cordelette. If it's a new route, bring a lot. On alpine climbs, forget leaving biners and rap rings- you're not going to top-rope the rap-off! See the bolting and anchor section for retro fitting rappel chains.

If you're going for it as fast and light as possible, you can tie your own runners out of $9/16^{th}$ inch webbing for leading, and then and use them as tat on the descent.

CARABINEERS

Keylocking Biners

Keylocks work well for rabbit runners and daisy chains (use a locking keylock) because they don't snag when you are unclipping. Just to clarify, keylock does not mean the biner is a locker, but that the nose of the biner is rounded and fits in the gate like a lock.

Wiregates

Use lightweight wire gates for slings and gear. Bring one biner per cam if it's hard climbing, otherwise combine 2-3 similar sized cams per biner. If you've double cams up, make sure you've got enough biners on your slings. The lightest wiregates on the market so far were made by CAMP, but Metolius has come out with an insanely small biner. These tiny carabineers are difficult to use with gloves however. The Black Diamond OZ carabiners are excellent lightweight wiregates, and they have a larger opening. Smaller opening biners are nice for the rack to keep things nice and compact. Keep the larger gated biners for the rope end of your slings and for ice-climbing with gloves on.

Lightweight Lockers

Locking carabiners (keylocks if possible) are necessary for daisy chains, the rope side of an auto-locking belay device, and your regular belay device. Trango makes the lightest ones so far. Keep an eye on your belay device locker for rope abrasions. Since they are so light, the rope can leave quite the groove in these in a short amount of time. Use your heavier auto-locking carabiners for general cragging to spare the wear and tear on your lightweight biners.

PROTECTION

Nuts (Stoppers)

For most routes keep one set of nuts on a non-keylock style wire gate to keep the nuts from falling off. Bring a #3 up to a #10 Black Diamond (or similar) size, plus two extra of the small/mid rage (#6-8 Black Diamond). Adding Four to five HB offsets (now made by DMM as aluminum nuts) or micro nuts in the med-large range (cover #1-5 nut size) covers your bases for thin cracks, and bring more if it's really thin and hard. For easy to moderate alpine bring one each #4-#10 Black Diamond or equivalent. Cams usually fit in the bigger nut sizes and are much quicker to place and clean than nuts, however, nuts are much lighter and replaceable than cams.

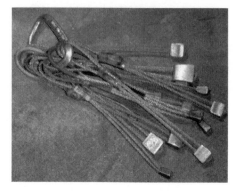

Cams

There are a ton of camming devices on the market, some good, some bad. Black Diamond set the new standard with their Camalots, and it is my opinion that size .5 and up are the best cams out there, although Wild County's #7 Flexible Friend is lighter and more stable than a #5 Camalot (DMM will be unveiling a new cam modeled off the Camalot, but lighter.) Below that size of cam, I prefer the new Metolius Master Cams. I believe they have successfully replaced Aliens as the small cam of choice, and have now introduced offset Master Cams. Wild Country Zero's pick up the slack in the ridiculously tiny sizes for aid and psychological pro in the #1-3 sizes. What's important is that you are comfortable with the cam and its sizes, and that the cam will hold a fall. Instead of hours of re-creating internet bickering threads on what's the best cam, I'm just going to use what I like.

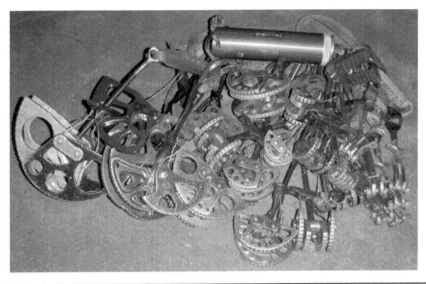

In general, if the climbing is very easy, or if you are on an ice route with very few mixed ice sections just bring about 5 cams (finger to fist size). If it's moderately easy climbing or fully mixed (let's just say for argument hard 5.7 to easy 5.9), bring one set of cams up from a yellow Metolius Master Cam (or equivalent) size to a #3 blue Camalot (or equivalent) size, and also two to three extra in the size you think you'll need (#.5 purple Camalot through #1 red Camalot are always useful). This should total 6-7 cams.

If it's harder climbing, then bring the above mentioned rack, plus doubles in the 0.5-2 Camalot or equivalent size (and extra bigger stuff if only if the route calls for it), and also tack on one purple, two blue, another yellow, and one orange (or equivalent) Metolius Master Cam sizes. You probably don't need a rack this big for mixed routes. If it's really hard or sustained thin climbing bring an extra blue and purple Metolius Master Cam sizes each, plus a grey Master Cam or equivalent. On rock first ascents I like to bring two larger ultra light cams that are equal to the Camalot (new sizes) #4 and #6 just in case.

There are many companies that make cams lighter and cover larger ranges than Black Diamond and Metolius, so shop around and go with what you feel comfortable leading with. Make sure your partner is comfortable with your cam selection as well. Wild Country Zeros are the smallest cams around and Valley Giants are the biggest made.

Aliens and some other cams DO NOT WORK in freezing conditions, especially when ice and snow covered. Use Metolius TCUs, Master Cams, or Black Diamond C3's instead. Give your axels a good does of lube before you go (graphite is the best choice) and clean them too.

Pins

Generally you don't need pins on established rock routes. On mixed alpine routes and first ascents, they are priceless. Titanium pins are light and awesome, but don't bring them on a popular route since you probably won't get them back out. On a mixed route or an FA bring a mix of 2-5 knifeblades, bugaboos, and lost arrows, plus 1-2 small angles. Small to mid sizes are best, and bugaboos are the most useful of these pitons. If small cam can fit where a bigger pin would, you don't need a pin that wide. 1-2 inches in length works well.

Ice axe picks work as a pin in a tight spot. I like to keep a RURP, a Black Diamond Talon hook, a medium sized Leeper Cam Hook, and/or a Black Diamond Specter on my "hail Mary" biner (my Loweballs, Tricams, and maybe a Snarg or piece of conduit are on there too depending on the route). Don't forget to bring a hammer for you and your partner each when bringing pins!

Tri-Cams

Tri-cams can fit when nothing else will. They are perfect on alpine routes because they are lighter than cams, or routes that specifically call for them (limestone pockets are an example). I suggest bringing the three choice sizes: Pink, Red, and Brown. They are lighter than a camming device, and if placed properly, work just as well. The major downside is that they can be a total pain to get out, and can easily become fixed pieces of gear.

One way to make Tri-Cams easier to place, and easier to clean is to wrap the nylon sling just above the clip-loop and up to the head of the cam in duct-tape. This "stiffens" the tri-cam and doesn't really add much weight or bulk.

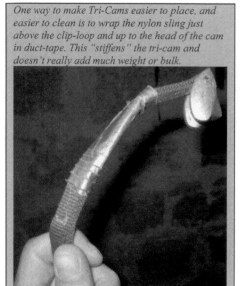

Russian Titanium Fly-Wheel Segment – The original TriCam! Found on Inspiration Peak North Face 2007. Placed in 1977.

Loweballs and Slider Nuts.

These babies are sweet for mixed routes or insanely thin cracks you don't want to nail. Grab two of the smallest sizes. They are extremely difficult to remove if overset or fallen on and are not meant to hold huge falls.

Big Bros

Only bring these if you are certain you're going to need them. Most cams cover all but the last two Big Bro sizes, so it makes sense to just get the biggest of the big bros. Make sure you know how to place them before running out that next offwidth!

Emergency Bolt Kit

If the rock type and climbing warrants it, bring along a small hand drill, hammer, and some bolts. If you're not putting up a classic, sketchy buttonheads or ¼ inch bolts with or without hangers will suffice as an emergency kit. Shown here are Fred Beckey's hand drill, a ZMac bolt, a ¼ inch bolt, a bomber 3/8 inch bolt, a lightweight rusty rivet hanger, and a heavier regular hanger. Standard bolting technique and equipment is covered in the Bolting section.

Fred Beckey's Bolt Kit

ICE PROTECTION

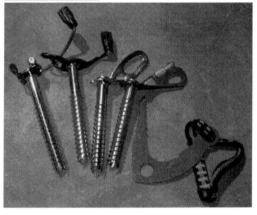

Ice Screws

Alpine ice routes generally don't take screws very well. I've never placed more than 3 screws on a route in one alpine ice pitch. One is acceptable, but if the route is something like a massive hard ice apron, then bring up to six. If the climb is pure water ice near, or at your limit, then 11 total screws (2 for each anchor, 7 for the lead) is a good number. Sizes of screws change as manufactures modify screws, but around five 17cm (4 for belays one for your best piece) and six 13cm is a good bet to bring. 22cm are useless for most climbs, but bring one for v-threads or to beef the belay in fat ice if you're worried about the anchors holding. Bring one or two 10cm screws if it's supposed to be a thin route (still keeping your number of screws at 11). Grivel 360 screws are the best for quickly placing a screw in an area that you don't want to spend time clearing out a space for the hanger.

You can slot screws behind ice curtains, straight down on a fractured pillar, or pound them in cracks if things get desperate.

> *It's worth it to get your ice screws, picks, and crampons professionally sharpened every so often. Check out www.grizguides.com for their rates on sharpening your hardware.*

Flukes
Snow flukes are not normally useful, but have their place in snow too soft for pickets, or for crevasse rescue. Mine collects dust on the shelf.

Deadmen
Bury essentially anything in the right snow conditions, and it can be a totally bomber anchor or piece of pro. In horrific snow conditions, I have slung and buried my entire backpack on lead (much to the excitement of my partner who had to carry it back up!).

Specters
These pound-in ice picks are useful in turf or poor ice, and can be hammered into cracks like pitons. They are also useful for mud climbing in the desert!

Snargs
Snargs are old-school pound-ins that work great in crappy ice or turf, (but you may have to steal them from the display case at the local mountaineering museum). They are a complete pain in the butt to clean, but it's nice to have on for bailing off of just in case.

Electrical Conduit
Conduit is still useful as a last resort anchor or rappel piece in horrid ice (especially rime-ice) conditions, but don't let anyone see you use it!

Pickets
These are super useful. On a very steep and unprotectable alpine faces you could use 4-5! I normally bring 2-3 on an alpine ice and snow routes. Both you and your partner should have one handy for glacier travel. One philosophy is that if it's terrain you can place a picket in, then you don't need to put pro in. I disagree completely. Sometimes they are the only thing keeping you on the mountain. On easy terrain just before a steep run-out section, you'll be really glad you put a picket in. Bring one biner on a sling girth hitched for each picket.

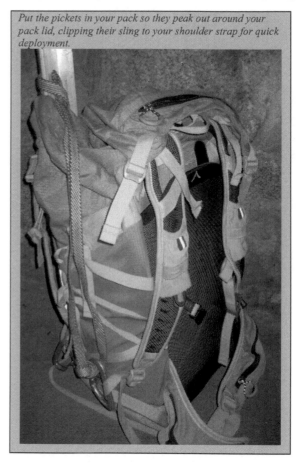

Put the pickets in your pack so they peak out around your pack lid, clipping their sling to your shoulder strap for quick deployment.

Warthogs
These babies are the pro of choice for turf protection and bullet hard alpine ice. Mountain Technology out of the U.K. has brought these previously impossible to find back on the market. Go to www.needlesports.com to buy them.

Russian Titanium Screw
You would think these would be excellent expensive screws, right? Although they are really light, the Russian Ti-screws go in horribly and are really cheap. In other words, they make great screws to rappel off of and leave behind. Put on one the back of your harness with a leaver biner.

202

Ice-Tools, Hammers, and Crampons

Hammer

If there's no ice and you need a hammer, buy a tiny cheap wooden hammer at the hardware store and sling the head with some webbing. Make sure the leash on your piton driving hammer is strong, but cheap webbing. Keep a free tosser biner on it that you will never use for anything but removing pins and bailing off of. It's hard to get away with just one hammer between the two people, so both partners need one. You'll want a full-on wall hammer for aid routes and putting up bolted climbs.

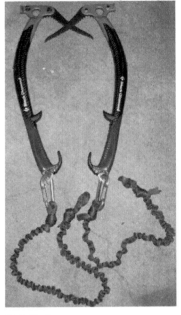

Ice Tools

Leashless Ergo are great for hard water ice and mixed routes but can get in the way on lower angled terrain. Regular leashed tools are easier to plunge and are a good choice on less technical big mountain routes. Leashless (non-ergo grip) ice tools are the most versatile modern ice tool. Leashless tools are great and if you don't have them yet, you should!

Russian ice tools are great devices for running up terrain quickly. These tools are essential picks with handles, so most of the technique is "high dagger" versus a full swing. Grivel makes this pair shown.

Umbilicals

Attach an umbilical cord system to your leashless tools by using scrunched up supertape and elastic. Fishing supply stores are a great place to find a swivel to keep the lines from twisting. Black Diamond makes the only commercially available umbilicals at the moment unless you can get a hold of Grivel who no longer serves North America. Don't bother with umbilicals on low-commitment short routes you could easily bail off with just one tool.

Illumination Rock, OR

3rd Tool and Wall Hammer

I have a children's ice tool with a hammer, The Simond Fox. Grivel makes a stamped thin metal mini version of their Monster tool that should work great. Use the 3rd tool for your glacier travel ax as well as your third tool on ice routes – you don't need a mountaineering ax unless you're only doing walk-ups. If you're going bring pins, you need a hammer, and more times than not on a rock route where you need pins, you need an ice ax too. See the hammer tips earlier in this chapter.

If you don't need pins and you're not doing an extended glacier travel session, you can use a large rock, larger Cam, or a trekking pole for self arresting instead, but be careful! Nut tools won't stop you (I know).

Parts

Have hammers on both tools. Have one tool with an adz if it's going to be a long snowy climb with lots of chopping involved. Bring a spare pick and a wrench to attach the pick (the pick can also be used as a piton in a pinch) on longer routes. Also bring a little file that's easily accessible to sharpen your points during the climb.

I keep my little file, spare pick, wrench, v-threader, Russian-Ti screw, a knife, and a small length of tat on a leaver biner clipped to the back of my harness so I never forget them.

CRAMPONS

For anything but steep waterfall or mixed, horizontal point crampons work best: Black Diamond and Petzl both make aggressive horizontal point crampons.

For steep ice use vertical points to maximize security, and for mixed or very steep ice use monopoint crampons. Both are a matter of taste so this is just a general rule. Some mixed climbers love dual points, and some pure-ice climbers love monopoints. For summer alpine use 16oz aluminum strap-ons over your tennis shoes. For some reason, strap-on crampon manufacturers don't realize people are using these on tennis/approach shoes with a much narrower forefoot. The result is your toes are forced through the front bail, sometimes reaching the ends of the front-points! Let's get with the program crampon makers!

Sometimes you can get away with only one pair of crampons. To do this, either just wear one crampon per partner, or if the section you need crampons for is less than 200 feet, have one person lead up, tie the crampons to the end of the rope and huck them down (or the second can "Batman" up the rope sans crampons).

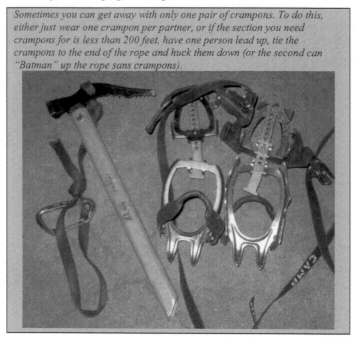

GLACIER TRAVEL RIG

For a crevasse rescue set-up, you'll need a Texas kick-step prusik, a chest prusik, a sling for your pack, two locking biners for your harness, 0-2 pulleys, 0-2 Tiblocs or Ropemen, and a picket and or fluke with biners each. You will also need about 4-6 biners for the prusiks, pulleys and anchors. Be sure and practice your glacier rig, and especially how to set-up a two person 6 to 1 Z-drag pulley system, and how to prusik out of a crevasse.

> *If you are climbing rock or ice after the crevasse section, see what climbing gear can be used for both your glacier rig, and your rock/ice rig. A cordelette can be converted into a Texas kick-step prusik, and slings can be used as prusik as well (using a Bachman's or Klemheist knot). Read up and practice your systems.*

AID EQUIPMENT

For moderate amounts of aid climbing, bring a pair of lightweight alpine aiders, two jumar-style ascenders, and two daisy chains. Lightweight adjustable daisys are available to help speed things up. Bring a fifi-hook if you're used to using one. If the climb is mostly moderate to difficult aid, you're going to want to bring beefier equipment than some mentioned in this text, plus extra aid climbing gizmos. See the French free section for info on short sections of aid. Kong is coming up with a slick looking jumar system that looks very lightweight.

Storm Mountain, UT

RECOMMENDED READING

There are tons of books out there you can read and learn about the myriad aspects of climbing and mountain travel. Listed below are the books I think are the best on their subject matter, and that cover subjects in much more detail than the scope of this book allows without being redundant. Also listed are some helpful websites.

http://sites.google.com/site/climbingstronger - The website for this book with updates and new information
American Alpine Journal: www.americanalpineclub.org/aajsearch - Online American Alpine Journal search engine.
www.avalanche.org - Links to local avalanche and weather forecasts.
Big Wall Climbing: Elite Technique, by Jared Ogden. Chris McNamara will be (hopefully) coming out soon with what should be an excellent aid and big wall how to book.
www.cascadeclimbers.com – A great resource for beta and spray for the Pacific NW. and just about everywhere else.
www.chirunning.com – A new philosophy in running technique.
www.chongonation.com - Chongo Chuck's aid climbing bible!
Climbing Anchors, by Craig Luebben. A great book for beginning Trad leaders.
Climbing Self-Rescue, by Andy Tyson and Molly Loomis. Knowing how to get yourself or your partner out of a bad situation is invaluable. A must read.
www.climbingweather.com. Type in where you want to climb and this site will pull up the weather from the exact GPS location from NOAA (www.weather.gov). Totally sweet!
CrossFit: www.crossfit.com - Tons of exercises for general and core conditioning.
Eat Drink and Be Healthy, by Walter Willett. A must read for those interested in nutrition.
Extreme Alpinism, by Mark Twight. The book that broke the mold. Required reading.
Fixing Your Feet, by John Vonhof. The bible on foot injuries.
www.grizguides.com – Professional tool, screw, and crampon sharpening service.
HealthNotes: http://library.gnc.com/healthnotes - Online peer-reviewed supplement resource accessed free via GNC.
Gym Jones: www.gymjones.com - Mark Twight's gym with great info and exercise routines
Ice & Mixed Climbing: Modern Technique, by Will Gadd. Excellent book for beginners and experienced climbers alike.
The Illustrated Guide to Glacier and Crevasse Rescue, by Tyson & Clelland. A must read for glacier travel.
Linus Pauling Institute http://lpi.oregonstate.edu/ - Hands down the best reference on vitamins and minerals
Medicine for Mountaineering, by James Wilkerson. The best first aid book out there for climbers.
Mountain Athlete: www.mtnathlete.com - Like Crossfit and Gym Jones, but more specific to climbing.
Mountaineering: The Freedom of the Hills. This is the must have for folks learning to climb, or for experienced climbers who need to brush up on particular skills. Excellent map, compass, and mountain travel sections for beginners or brushing up.
Northwest Mountaineering Journal: www.mountaineers.org/nwmj. Details on new route activity in the Pacific Northwest.
Mountain Project: www.mountainproject.com – Quickly becoming an online guidebook to the planet. Excellent source of beta and conditions as well.
http://www.nal.usda.gov/fnic/foodcomp/search/- USDA's website will give you a total nutritional breakdown of the foods you enter
Northwest Mountain Weather, by Jeff Renner. A great book on learning about predicting weather in the backcountry. Not just for Pacific Northwesterners.
www.posetech.com – Like Chi Running, another leap forward in running technique
Practical Programming For Strength Training, by Mark Rippetoe and Lon Kilgore. A companion book to the excellent "Starting Strength".
Rock Climbing: Mastering Basic Skills, by Craig Luebben. This is the best how to rock climb book for beginners I've seen to date.
Rock Warriors Way, by Arno Ilgner. An absolute must for all climbers. Mental training is just as, if not more, important than the physical training.
The Self Coached Climber, by Dan Hague and Douglas Hunter. A great book on climbing movement.
Starting Strength, by Mark Rippetoe and Lon Kilgore. The best recourse out there for general strength training.
Staying Alive In Avalanche Terrain, by Bruce Tremper. Required reading for everyone who travels in the winter backcountry.
Training For Climbing, by Eric Horst. Excellent description of finger strength training, including the H.I.T. Technique which Horst developed.

ABOUT THE AUTHOR

Dr. Layton has been climbing alpine rock and ice routes for almost twenty years, including many first ascents in Alaska, British Columbia, Nevada, Oregon, Utah, and Washington. He has appeared in Alpinist, Climbing, and Rock & Ice magazines for his first ascents and climbing accomplishments. He was the recipient of the 2006 Fred Beckey Award for several bold first ascents, including what was called "the most significant climb [in the Pacific Northwest] in the past 50 years," on the East Face of Mox Peak, just days after completing a Grade 6 first ascent on the other side of the state.

Dr. Layton received his Doctor of Chiropractic from Western States Chiropractic College in Portland, OR and received his Bachelor's in Exercise Science from Western Washington University in Bellingham, WA. Michael is a recent transplant to Salt Lake City, Utah. When he's not climbing, skiing, or running, he owns a small rehabilitation clinic helping athletes and families recover from injuries and stay healthy. He also works for the University of Utah (ARUP Laboratories) sequencing and analyzing DNA of infectious and esoteric diseases. Finally, Dr. Layton works as an advisor for insurance companies, substitute teaches, and self-publishes books when he feels the need to punish himself for climbing too much.

Wayne Wallace Photo

Wayne Wallace Photo

THE END!

Chilliwack Range, BC
Jay Hack Photo

cilo gear
ETHICS = ACTION

www.cilogear.com

METOLIUS

www.metoliusclimbing.com

WILD
COUNTRY ™

Always Leading

ph. John Evans

People. Passion. Adventure. **PETZL**®

Michael Fuselier / Swingline / 5.13d / Red River Gorge, KY

Made in the USA
Charleston, SC
11 January 2010